Business Vocabulary in Use

Elementary

Bill Mascull

CAMBRIDGE
UNIVERSITY PRESS

CAMBRIDGE UNIVERSITY PRESS
Cambridge, New York, Melbourne, Madrid, Cape Town, Singapore, São Paulo

Cambridge University Press
The Edinburgh Building, Cambridge CB2 2RU, UK

www.cambridge.org
Information on this title: www.cambridge.org/9780521606219

© Cambridge University Press 2006

First published 2006

Printed in Italy by Printer Trento Srl

A catalogue record for this publication is available from the British Library

ISBN–13 978-0-521-60621-9 Student's Book
ISBN–10 0-521-60621-7 Student's Book

Produced by Kamae Design
Cover design by Dale Tomlinson
Illustrations by Clinton Banbury, Phil Garner and Kamae Design

Contents

MONEY

PRODUCTS AND SERVICES

SOCIALIZING

Introduction

Who is this book for?

Business Vocabulary in Use Elementary is in the same series as *Business Vocabulary in Use Intermediate* and *Advanced*. It is designed to help you to learn basic business vocabulary. It also helps you to learn the language of business communication for social situations, telephone calls, business writing, presentations, and meetings.

The book is for people who are studying English before they start work, and for people already working who need English for their job.

You can use the book on your own for self-study, or with a teacher in the classroom.

What is in the book?

In the book there are 49 two-page units.

The first three units are **learner training** units. They give you ideas on the best ways to learn. They explain the instructions used in the book, how to do the exercises, how to learn vocabulary and how to use dictionaries. It is a good idea to do these units first to help you use the rest of the book in the best way.

There are then two units about how to use **numbers**.

After that, there are 28 **subject units** with key vocabulary for different business subjects, and 16 units with **business communication** language. These help you with the **skills** you need in business, for example in presentations and meetings.

The new words and expressions for you to learn in each unit are in **bold**. They are explained in different ways, for example with a sentence showing you how to use them, or with pictures. Sometimes there is a '=' symbol, followed by some words to explain the new language.

You can use the **contents** pages at the beginning of the book to find the subject or skill that you want to study.

There is an **answer key** at the back of the book. Most of the exercises have questions with only one correct answer. But in some of the exercises, including the **Over to you** activities at the end of each unit (see below), you write and/or talk about yourself and your own organization. So the answers in the key for these sections are examples, to compare with your own answers.

There is also an **index**. This is a list of the new words and expressions in the book and the unit numbers where they appear. The index also tells you how to say the words and expressions.

The left-hand page

This page shows the new words and expressions for each subject or skills area. Each page has a number of sections with the letters A, B, C (and sometimes D), and short titles.

On the left-hand page there is:

- information about the meanings of the words and expressions.
- information about word combinations - words that are often used together.
- notes on language points such as the differences between British and American English.
- notes to tell you where you can find more information in other units.

The right-hand page

The exercises on the right-hand page give you practice in using the new words and expressions shown on the left-hand page. There are different types of exercise for this. Sometimes the exercise asks you to write sentences, or to write words to finish sentences. Some units contain tables or diagrams to complete, or crosswords.

'Over to you' activities

An important part of *Business Vocabulary in Use Elementary* is the **Over to you** activity at the end of each unit. The **Over to you** activities give you the chance to practise the words and expressions from the unit in a way that is useful in your own job or studies.

Self-study learners can do this section as a written activity.

In the classroom, the teacher can use the **Over to you** exercises for discussion with the whole class, or in small groups. After the discussion the teacher can ask learners to look again at the words and expressions that have caused difficulty. Learners can then do the **Over to you** exercise as a written activity, for example as homework.

How to use the book for self-study

Find the subject or word that you are looking for in the contents page or the index. Read the information on the left-hand page of the unit. Do the exercises on the right-hand page. Check your answers in the key. If you have made mistakes, go back and look at the unit again. Note down important words and expressions in your notebook.

How to use the book in the classroom

Teachers can choose units that relate to learners' needs or interests, for example areas they have covered in course books, or that have come up in other activities. Alternatively, lessons can contain a regular vocabulary slot, where learners look at the vocabulary of particular subject or skills areas.

Learners can work on the units individually or in pairs or groups, with the teacher going round the class assisting and advising. Teachers should get learners to think about the logical process of the exercises, pointing out why one answer is possible and the others are not.

We hope you enjoy using this book.

1 Talking about language

A Grammar words used in this book

Grammar word	Meaning	Example
noun	a person or thing	*director, job*
singular	one person or thing	*executive, office*
plural	more than one person or thing	*executives, offices*
adjective	describes a person or thing	*friendly, heavy*
adverb	describes a verb: how something is done	*usually, often*
preposition	used before a noun or pronoun	*in, on, with, for*
verb	something that a person or thing does – often an action	*work, make*
base form (= infinitive)	the first form of the verb, used with 'to'	*to make* *It's easy to make a mistake.*
second form (= past simple)	the verb form that you use to talk about the past	*She went to school in Liverpool.*
third form (= past participle)	the verb form that you use in the present perfect tense, and in passives	*I've learnt a lot in this job.* *It was developed by IBM.*
question	a set of words to ask for information	*Where does she work?*
answer	a reply to a question	*She works in an office.*
phrase	a group of words, not a complete sentence	*an interesting job*
sentence	a complete idea. In writing, it starts with a capital letter and ends with a full stop.	*He is very good with computers.*
expression	a word or group of words used in a special situation	*I'll put you through.*

To learn more about verbs, see pages 107–113.

B Understanding notes in this book

vowels = the letters *a*, *e*, *i*, *o*, and *u*
consonants = all other letters
BrE = British English

AmE = American English
formal = for public or official use
informal = not official; used with friends or colleagues

C Understanding instructions in this book

Complete the table. = Fill in the spaces in the table with information. (For example, exercise 27.1)

Complete the sentences. = Write the missing words. (For example, exercise 5.1)

Match the two parts of the sentences. = Join the two parts to make a whole sentence. (For example, exercise 18.2)

True or false? = Is this right or wrong? (For example, exercise 9.1)

Choose the correct word to complete each sentence. = Choose the right word to use in the sentence. (For example, exercise 24.2)

Look at A/B/C opposite to help you. = Look at section A/B/C to find the information that you need to do the exercise. (For example, exercise 4.3)

Put the sentences into the correct order. = Say which sentence is first, which is second, etc. (For example, exercise 43.3)

1.1   Write the grammar words in A opposite in your language.

1.2   Look at B opposite. Write the instructions in your own language.

1.3   Write the words in the box in the correct column in the table.

| big | expensive | helpful | job | learn | long |
| lose | money | old | salary | sales | sell |

Noun	Verb	Adjective
job		

1.4   Are these phrases, sentences, or questions? Look at A opposite to help you.

1 Do you get the train to work?   *question*
2 on the bus
3 He went to school in London.
4 good with computers
5 I'm an architect.
6 a part-time job

1.5   True or false? Look at A opposite to help you.

1 The plural of 'office' is 'offices'.   *True*
2 'was' and 'were' are the past forms of 'be'.
3 'on' is a preposition.
4 'cheap' is an adverb.
5 'sometimes' is an adverb.
6 'Can we meet on Monday?' is a phrase.

1.6   Follow these instructions.

1 Complete the sentence.

I live .... Paris.

2 Complete the table. Look at page 112 to help you.

Base form (infinitive)	Second form (past simple)
be	was/were
become	
	came

3 Match the two parts of the sentences. Look at A opposite to help you.

1 A noun is a word	a that describes a verb.
2 An adverb is a word	b that describes a person or thing.
3 An adjective is a word	c for a person or a thing.

4 Choose the correct word to complete each sentence. Look at A, B and C opposite to help you.

1 The .... (base/second) form is the infinitive of the verb.
2 You use the .... (first/second) form of the verb to talk about the past.
3 You use the .... (singular/plural) when you talk about more than one person or thing.
4 A .... (question/sentence) is a set of words used to ask for information.
5 A .... (phrase/expression) is a set of words that is not a complete sentence.

2 Learning vocabulary

To help you remember vocabulary, keep a vocabulary notebook. Write the words that you learn from this book in it.

A Word combinations

You **do exercises** in this book. Sometimes, you **make mistakes**.

Words used together are **word combinations**. To help you remember word combinations, write in your vocabulary book: **do an exercise** and **make a mistake**.

Word combinations show you which words can go in front of another word, and which words can go after it. More examples of word combinations:

verb + preposition: I **work in** the sales department. (Unit 43)

noun + noun: **company car, company restaurant, company pension** (Unit 25)

verb + noun:

arrange miss cancel	a meeting

B Learn words in families

The units are organized to help you learn words and phrases in families.

Word family	Some words in the family		
describing a product	light	fast	easy to use
describing a service	friendly	reliable	helpful

C Pictures and diagrams

Draw pictures to help you remember words.

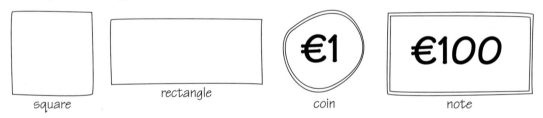

square   rectangle   coin   note

Draw diagrams like this one. Put more words in the diagrams as you learn them.

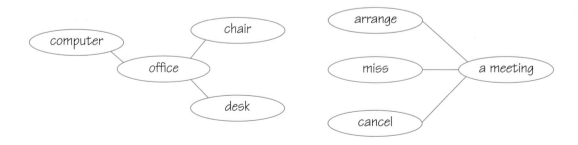

2.1 Choose the words from the box that can go in front of 'job'. Look at Unit 8 to help you.

full-time	part-time	sometimes	overtime	permanent	contract	employee

2.2 Complete the table with words and phrases from the box.

research and development	cash	marketing	currency	training	dollars

Word family	Some words in the family
money	cash
company departments	

2.3 Match the words to the pictures.

1 photographer (Unit 6)
2 factory (Unit 7)
3 change money (Unit 22)
4 load (Unit 29)
5 fall (Unit 45)
6 rise (Unit 45)

a

b

c

d

e

f

2.4 Complete the diagram. Look at A opposite to help you.

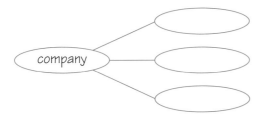

company

3 Using a dictionary

What dictionaries do I need?

You should use two dictionaries: a good **bilingual dictionary** (= English and your own language) and a good **English–English dictionary**, like the *Cambridge Essential English Dictionary*.

The bilingual dictionary is easier to understand, but the English–English dictionary can give you more information about a word or phrase. It's good to work in English as much as possible.

What information does a dictionary give?

Each **entry** gives:

- the meaning(s). Sometimes there is more than one meaning.
- the pronunciation (= the way that you say a word) using the phonetic alphabet.
- grammar information (if the word is a noun, verb, adjective, adverb, etc.).
- example phrases or sentences.
- common word combinations and expressions (in the *Cambridge Essential English Dictionary* these are in **bold**).
- words with opposite meaning, if there are any.

---

company /ˈkʌmpənɪ/ *noun*

1 (*plural* **companies**) an organisation which sells things or services: *a software company*

2 [**no plural**] when you have a person or people with you: *I enjoy his company.*

A dictionary entry

How should I use my dictionary?

Here are some ideas to help you.

- Many words have more than one meaning. The first meaning is not always the one that you want. Look at all the different meanings.
- When you look up a word, put a ✓ next to it. When you go back to the page later and see the ✓, check that you remember the word without looking at the meaning.
- If you see an English word in a text, try to guess the meaning and continue to read. Then use your dictionary to check the meaning.
- If you look up an English word in a bilingual dictionary and find several different words in your own language, look up the English word in an English–English dictionary to find the right meaning.

Use the *Cambridge Essential English Dictionary (CEED)*, or another English–English dictionary, to do these exercises.

3.1 Answer the questions.

1 In *CEED*, the entries for words beginning with 'A' use 21 pages. What letter of the alphabet uses the most pages? How many pages does it use?

....

2 What letter of the alphabet has the smallest number of entries? How many entries are there?

....

3 What entry comes before 'employee'? What entry comes after it?

....

4 'rose' is the past tense of a verb. If you want to find out which verb, where in the dictionary do you look?

....

5 Put these entries in alphabetical order: 'worker', 'worth', 'work', 'worse', 'world', 'World Wide Web'.

....

3.2 Look at the entry for 'heavy'.

1 How many meanings are there?

....

2 Write the word in the phonetic alphabet.

....

3 Is it a noun, a verb, or an adjective?

....

4 What is its opposite?

....

3.3 Look at the entry for 'job'.

1 Can you use this word in the plural?

....

2 What example phrases and sentences are there?

....

3 In which expressions can you use 'job'?

....

4 Can you use these expressions in American English?

....

3.4 Look at the entry for 'business'.

1 Is it a noun, a verb, or an adjective?

....

2 How many meanings does it have?

....

3 What example phrases and sentences are there?

....

4 Numbers and years

Zero to ninety-nine

0	zero, nought, oh						
1	one	6	six	11	eleven	16	sixteen
2	two	7	seven	12	twelve	17	seventeen
3	three	8	eight	13	thirteen	18	eighteen
4	four	9	nine	14	fourteen	19	nineteen
5	five	10	ten	15	fifteen	20	twenty
21	twenty-one	43	forty-three	65	sixty-five	87	eighty-seven
30	thirty	50	fifty	70	seventy	90	ninety
32	thirty-two	54	fifty-four	76	seventy-six	98	ninety-eight
40	forty	60	sixty	80	eighty	99	ninety-nine

> BrE: zero, nought, oh; AmE: zero

B **Larger numbers**

	BrE	AmE
100	a hundred	one hundred
120	a hundred and twenty one hundred and twenty	one hundred twenty
200	two hundred	

1,000	a thousand one thousand
1,250	one thousand two hundred and fifty — one thousand two hundred fifty
12,000	twelve thousand
55,000	fifty-five thousand
350,000	three hundred and fifty thousand — three hundred fifty thousand

1,000,000	a million one million
1,000,000,000	a billion one billion

Note: For 1,000 and above, you use commas to separate the figures into groups of three, starting from the right (for example, 10,000,000). You don't use full stops or other punctuation.

C **Years**

You say years like this:

1789	seventeen eighty-nine
1800	eighteen hundred
1805	eighteen oh five
1969	nineteen sixty-nine
2000	two thousand
2001	two thousand and one (BrE), two thousand one (AmE)
2009	two thousand and nine (BrE), two thousand nine (AmE)

> The French Revolution was **in 1789**.

> Astronauts landed on the moon **in 1969**.

To learn more about work and numbers, see Unit 9; time, Unit 15; money, Unit 21.

4.1 Match the facts to the numbers.

1 the number of metro stations in Paris ——— 240,000
2 the number of miles from the earth to the moon   191
3 the number of members of the United Nations ——432
4 the number of bicycles in Beijing   6,912
5 the number of languages in the world   11,000,000

4.2 Write the numbers in 4.1 above in words, in British English and American English.

two hundred and forty thousand (BrE), two hundred forty thousand (AmE)

4.3 Write the years in words. Look at C opposite to help you.

1 The first steam engine – 1698   Sixteen ninety-eight
2 The first railway locomotive – 1814
3 The first telephone – 1870
4 The first radio – 1901
5 The first television – 1926
6 The first computer – 1944
7 The World Wide Web – 1992

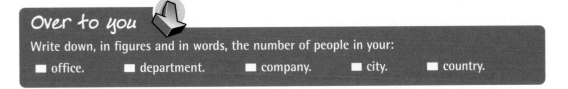

Over to you

Write down, in figures and in words, the number of people in your:
■ office.   ■ department.   ■ company.   ■ city.   ■ country.

5 Ordering numbers, parts of numbers

A   Ordering numbers

When you talk about the **order** of numbers, you use:

1st*	first	6th	sixth	11th	eleventh	16th	sixteenth
2nd*	second	7th	seventh	12th	twelfth	17th	seventeenth
3rd*	third	8th	eighth	13th	thirteenth	18th	eighteenth
4th	fourth	9th	ninth	14th	fourteenth	19th	nineteenth
5th	fifth	10th	tenth	15th	fifteenth	20th	twentieth

21st*	twenty-first	40th	fortieth	80th	eightieth
22nd*	twenty-second	50th	fiftieth	90th	ninetieth
23rd*	twenty-third	60th	sixtieth	100th	(one) hundredth
30th	thirtieth	70th	seventieth	120th	(one) hundred and twenty

* Be careful with these forms.

BrE: ground floor; AmE: first floor

> This my **first job**. I work in an office on the **thirty-fourth floor**. The building is on **Fifth Avenue**.

To learn more about numbers and dates, see Unit 17.

B   Decimals, fractions and percentages

When you talk or write about parts of numbers, you can use **decimals**, **fractions** or **percentages**.

point nine; 0.9

Decimals

0.3	(zero) **point** three (nought) point three	12.93	twelve point nine three
1.5	one point five	59.367	fifty-nine point three six seven

BrE: (zero) point three, (nought) point three; AmE: (zero) point three

nine-tenths; 9/10

Fractions

1/3	a third one third	3/5	three-fifths
2/3	two-thirds	7/32	seven thirty-seconds

Be careful with:

1 1/4	one and a quarter
2 1/2	two and a half
8 3/4	eight and three quarters

BrE: a quarter;
AmE: a quarter, a fourth

> A fifth of the world's population lives in China.

ninety per cent;
90%

Percentages

10% ten **per cent**	17.5% seventeen point five per cent	99.99% ninety-nine point nine nine per cent

Note: You say 'point' and you write a dot (.) in a decimal number. You don't use a comma (,).

5.1 Complete the sentences. Look at A opposite to help you.

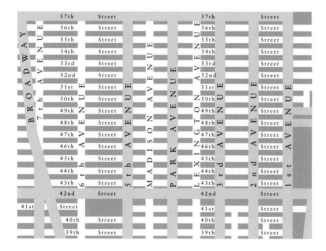

Office deliveries

Alain – 3rd

Birgit – 17th

Charlie – 29th

Davina – 33rd

Eddie – 41st

Francesca – 56th

1 Alain works on the ......*third*...... floor.
2 Birgit works on the .... floor.
3 Charlie works on the .... floor.
4 Davina works on the .... floor.
5 Eddie works on the .... floor.
6 Francesca works on the .... floor.

5.2 Mark the places on the map. Look at B opposite to help you.

1 United Nations – First Avenue and Forty-fourth Street
2 Times Square – Broadway and Forty-second Street
3 St Patrick's Cathedral – Fifth Avenue and Fiftieth Street
4 Carnegie Hall – Seventh Avenue and Fifty-seventh Street
5 Museum of Modern Art – Sixth Avenue and Fifty-third Street

5.3 Complete the table. Look at B opposite to help you.

	Percentage	Fraction	Decimal
1	...........*seventy-five per cent*...........	three quarters	....
2	....	....	(nought/zero) point five
3	twenty-five per cent	....	....
4	....	....	(nought/zero) point two
5	ten per cent	....	....

Over to you

Talk about the floors in the building where you work. Which floor do you work on, and which floors do your colleagues work on?

6 Jobs

Your job

What do you do? (= What is your job?)

I'm an engineer.

I'm an architect.

I'm a doctor.

I'm a photographer.

B Other jobs

What	does	he she Jim Maria	do?

What	do	they Linda and Pablo	do?

He's a construction worker.

She's a programmer.

She's an artist.

He's an oil worker.

He's a teacher.

She's a receptionist.

Maria's a personal assistant.

Jim's a tour guide.

They're teachers.

Note: You use 'a' in front of a consonant and 'an' in front of a vowel.

To learn more about the present simple, see page 107.

C Dream jobs

What's your dream job?

I want to be **a rock musician**.

6.1 Complete the sentences. Look at A opposite to help you.

1 I work on engines. I'm ……*an*…… *engineer* .
2 I take photos. I'm ………………… ……………… .
3 I design buildings. I'm ………………… ……………… .
4 I work in a hospital. I'm ………………… ……………… .

6.2 Match the pictures (1–6) to the jobs (a–f).

1

3

5

2

4

6

a a shop assistant   c a call centre worker   e a footballer
b a bus driver   d a teacher   f a barman

6.3 Write the questions for these answers.

1 *What* …*do*… *you* …*do*… ?
I'm a doctor.
2 ………… ………… ………… ………… ?
He's an architect.
3 ………… ………… ………… ………… ?
He's a barman and she's an oil worker.
4 ………… ………… ………… ………… ?
She's a policewoman.

Over to you

What do you do? What's your dream job?
Talk about the jobs of people that you know.

7 Places, departments and industries

A Places

Where do you work?

I work **in a factory**.

- in a shop
- in an office
- in a college
- at home
- **at head office** (= the most important office)

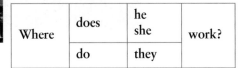

- on a construction site
- on a farm
- on an oil rig
- in Paris
- in Shanghai

Where	does	he she	work?
	do	they	

He She	works	on a farm.
They	work	

B Departments

Which department	does	he she	work in?
	do	you	

He **works in the sales department**. He sells the company's products.

She works **in the training department**. She organizes training courses.

I work **in the production department**. We make the company's products.

C Industries

You can talk about the **industry** that you work in like this:

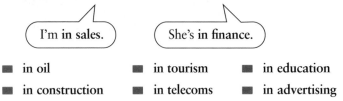

I'm **in sales.**

She's **in finance.**

- in oil
- in tourism
- in education
- in construction
- in telecoms
- in advertising

7.1 Match the two parts of what people say about their jobs. Look at A opposite to help you.

1 I work in the production department.   a I'm the boss!

2 I work in New York.   b I make televisions.

3 I work in a college.   c I sell machines.

4 I work at head office.   d I teach French.

5 I work in the sales department.   e I love big cities!

7.2 Complete the sentences with 'in', 'at' or 'on'. Look at B opposite to help you.

1 I work .... a shop.
2 I don't work .... a construction site.
3 I don't work .... home because I want to be with people all the time!
4 She works .... a factory.
5 He works .... the finance department.
6 They work .... a farm.
7 One day, I want to work .... head office. I want to be the boss!

7.3 Complete the questions. Look at A and B opposite to help you.

1 Which department .... ?
I work in the training department.

2 Which department .... ?
She works in the marketing department.

3 Which department .... ?
He works in the production department.

4 Where .... ?
I work at home.

5 Where .... ?
They work on an oil rig.

7.4 Complete each sentence with an industry. Look at C opposite to help you.

1 I work for Alcatel. I'm in ....
2 She works for Shell. She's in ....
3 He's a teacher. He's in ....
4 They're tour guides. They're in ....
5 We write advertisements. We're in ....
6 He builds houses. He's in ....

Over to you

Where do you work?

Talk about people you know – where do they work?

8 Types of work

Jobs and work

Charlotte Stone talks about BISG:

'I **work for** BISG, British International Stores Group. In our shops, we have **employees** (= people who work for our company) who have **full-time jobs**. Full-time employees usually work around 40 hours a week, but they can also do **overtime**, where they work longer and get more money.

Some employees have a **part-time job**. For example, some people work 20 hours a week.

Most people at BISG have a **permanent job** – they have no finish date.

Some people here do **temporary work** for a short period.

Every employee has a **contract**, an agreement about how long they work, when they work, etc.'

Note: You don't say 'a work'.

Stopping work

'When employees at BISG are 65, they **retire** (= stop work because of their age). They receive a good **pension** (= payment for people who retire).

If someone leaves the company, for example to move to another company, they **resign** (= tell the company they are leaving).

We **make** people **redundant** if we don't need them anymore – if we don't have work for them, or if we have financial problems.

If someone has done something wrong or stupid, then we **dismiss** or **fire** them (= ask them to leave the company).'

I work with ...

I work with people (= I help people every day in my job).

I work **with customers** (= people that buy our products).

I work **with suppliers** (= companies that we buy products from).

I work **with computers**.

I like my **colleagues** (= people that work with me).

8.1 Complete the crossword. Look at A and C opposite to help you.

Across

1 The people who buy your products are your .... (9)

7 I can work here as long as I want – I have a .... job. (9)

8 Your .... are the people that you work with. (10)

10 If you only work 20 hours a week, you work .... (4-4)

11 An agreement to work for a particular company. (8)

12 Today, most people need a .... to do their job. (8)

Down

2 If you work extra hours, you do .... (8)

3 .... are the companies we buy products from. (9)

4 I want to be a doctor because I like working with .... (6)

5 My job finishes next month – it's only .... (9)

6 I work 40 hours a week – it's a .... job. (4-4)

9 If you work for a company, you're an .... (8)

8.2 Complete the tables. Look at B opposite to help you.

Verb	Noun
	retirement
	resignation
	dismissal

Noun	Adjective
redundancy	

8.3 Complete the sentences with words from 8.2 above. Look at B opposite to help you.

1 There was no more work at the factory, so my company made me ....

2 I don't like what the company are doing, so I'm going to .... and find another job.

3 Pedro took money from the company, so they had to .... him.

4 When I .... , I'm going to read *War and Peace*.

Over to you

Think about your job or one that you would like to have. Is it a full-time job or a part-time job? Is it permanent or temporary?

9 Work and numbers

A How many employees are there?

Interviewer: **How many** employees **are there** at BISG?

Charlotte Stone: **Approximately** 4,000 – I think the **exact figure** is 4,053.

Interviewer: And how many shops are there?

Charlotte Stone: **There are** 34 shops in the UK and 22 in Europe.

Interviewer: **Is there** one in Paris?

Charlotte Stone: **Yes, there is.**

Interviewer: **Are there** many offices?

Charlotte Stone: **There's** (= there is) one head office and there are six other offices.

Interviewer: And how many **hours a week** do your employees work?

Charlotte Stone: The full-time employees work 42 hours a week **on average, including** overtime (= some work 40 hours a week and some work 44).

B Sites

Interviewer: **Where is** BISG's head office?

Charlotte Stone: BISG's **head office** is in London. About 70 people work there, **mostly** top managers (= 55 out of 70 are top managers).

Interviewer: How many other **sites** (= places with buildings) are there?

Charlotte Stone: Well, we have the other offices, the store **branches** (= different stores) and five other sites which are our **warehouses**. We keep the products there before they go to the stores.

Interviewer: So how many sites are there approximately?

Charlotte Stone: There are 7 offices, 56 branches and 5 warehouses, so there are approximately 70 sites **altogether**.

BISG

Head office – London

+ 6 offices

+ 56 branches   + 5 warehouses

= 68 sites (approximately 70)

To learn more about numbers, see Units 4, 15 and 21.

9.1 Look at the interviewer's notes about Singapore Computer Stores (SCS). Are the sentences below (1–4) true or false? Look at A and B opposite to help you.

Facts about SCS

Employees: 2,433

The London office has 30 employees (3 are managers).

Some employees work 46 hours a week, some work 44, and some 42.

10 offices

10 branches

One warehouse in London, one in Singapore

1 SCS has 22 sites altogether.
2 SCS has approximately 1,000 employees.
3 The people working at the London office are mostly managers.
4 Employees at SCS work 44 hours a week on average.

9.2 Complete the interview with Ann Lee, an SCS employee. Look at A and B opposite to help you.

Interviewer: (1) .... people work for SCS?
Ann Lee: It's not a big company. There are (2) .... 400 employees in Singapore and the UK – the (3) .... is 409.
Interviewer: And (4) .... branches are there?
Ann Lee: (5) .... seven branches in Singapore and three in the UK, so there are ten (6) ....
Interviewer: (7) .... two head offices, one in Singapore and one in London?
Ann Lee: No, (8) .... only one head office. It's in Singapore!
Interviewer: How many (9) .... do you work?
Ann Lee: Sometimes 40, sometimes 42, so (10) .... , I work 41 hours a week.

9.3 Choose the correct word to complete each sentence. Look at the diagram below and at C opposite to help you.

Summit Supermarkets

Frankfurt

 + 4

+ 90

+ 8

= 103

1 Summit Supermarkets is an international company with its .... (main office / head office) in Frankfurt as well as four other .... (branches / offices) in Europe.
2 We have a total of 90 .... (sites / branches) selling our products in Germany and Holland.
3 There are also eight .... (warehouses / sites) where we keep the products before we take them to the stores.
4 The company has 103 .... (offices / sites) altogether.

Over to you

Think about your organization or one you would like to work for. Where is its head office? Approximately how many employees are there? How many sites are there?

10 Getting to work

A Ways of getting to work

How do you get to work? (= How do you go to work?)

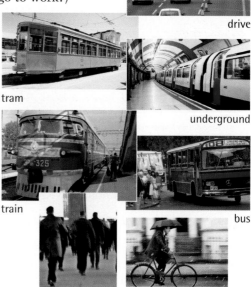

drive

I You We They	go by get the take the	tram. underground. train. bus.
	drive. walk. cycle.	

tram

underground

He She	goes by gets the takes the	tram. underground. train. bus.
	drives. walks. cycles.	

train

bus

walk   cycle

B Commuting

Samantha lives in Naseby and works in Osborne. Every day, she **commutes** (= travels to work) by train from Naseby to Osborne. She's a **commuter**.
She likes **commuting** – she does a lot of work on the train. A lot of her colleagues commute by car and by bus.

When you talk about commuting, you can say:

> I **leave home at** 8.00 and I **get to work at** 9.00.

Julia **leaves home at** 7.30 and she **gets to work at** 8.45.

Ed leaves work at 6.30 and he gets home at 8.00.

If the time is not the same every day, you can say:

I leave home at 8.00 and I **get to work at about** 9.00 (= get to work at 9.00, or just before or just after 9.00).

Julia leaves home at 7.30 and **she doesn't get to work before** 8.45 (= she gets to work at 8.45 or after 8.45).

Ed leaves work at 6.30 and he **never gets home before** 8.00 (= he gets home at 8.00 or after 8.00).

To learn more about the present simple, see page 107; time, Unit 15.

10.1 Match the two parts of what people say about getting to work. Look at A opposite to help you.

How do you get to work?

1 I get the train.

2 I walk.

3 I take the tram.

4 I don't cycle.

5 I drive.

6 I take the underground.

a I enjoy the fresh air.

b I can listen to music on the radio.

c It's dangerous and I don't like it when it rains.

d It stops just outside my house.

e It's hot down there in the summer!

f The station is near my house, and I can read on my way to work.

10.2 Complete the sentences using the correct verb forms. Look at B opposite to help you. Use the verb list on page 112 if you need more help.

1 Pierre .... (never get) home before 7.00.

2 He .... (not get) to work before 9.30.

3 He .... (leave) work at about 6.30.

4 He .... (go) home by metro. On the metro, he .... (read) *Le Monde*.

5 On his way to work, he .... (stop) at a café for a coffee.

6 Pierre .... (walk) to work. He likes the fresh air.

10.3 Put the steps (1–6) in 10.2 above into the correct order.

Over to you

How do you get to work? Do you commute? What time do you leave home? What time do you get to work?

11 Who's the boss?

A Managers and employees

This is part of the **organization chart** for Havajet, a company that makes planes. The **managers** are **in charge of** different activities. For example, the research and development director is in charge of developing products.

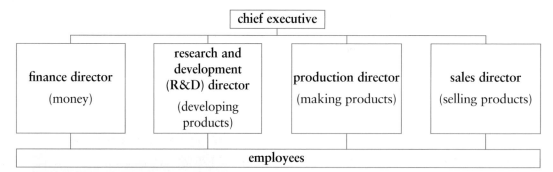

| chief executive |
| finance director (money) | research and development (R&D) director (developing products) | production director (making products) | sales director (selling products) |
| employees |

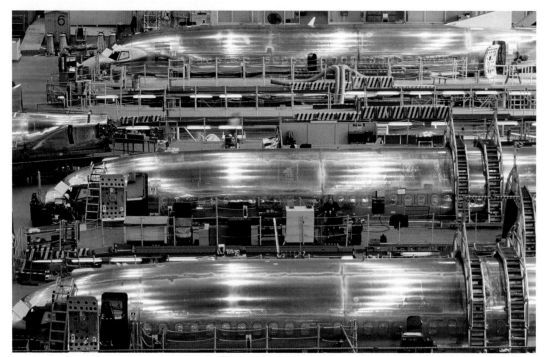

Note: **manager** = formal; **boss** = informal

B Managing departments

Miranda Thomas is **responsible for** sales at Havajet. There are 25 people who **work under** Miranda – 24 salespeople and her **personal assistant**, Julie. Julie helps Miranda with her work. For example, Julie is responsible for organizing Miranda's meetings.

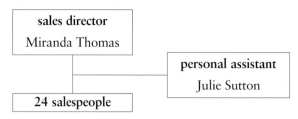

| sales director Miranda Thomas |
| personal assistant Julie Sutton |
| 24 salespeople |

11.1 Which managers at Havajet are in charge of the activities below? Look at A opposite to help you.

1 making the planes
the production director

2 getting the money to develop the planes

3 running the whole company

4 finding customers for the planes

5 thinking of new ideas for planes

11.2 Now write sentences with the same information as in 11.1 above, using 'responsible for'.

1 *The production director is responsible for making the planes.*

2

3

4

5

11.3 Draw an organization chart for the production department at Havajet, using the information below. Then write full sentences to describe the chart. Look at B opposite to help you.

- Carlos Sonera – production director
- four production managers
- one personal assistant – Sandy Baker
- 80 production workers

> **production director**
> Carlos Sonera

Carlos Sonera is in charge of production ...

Over to you

Draw an organization chart for your department.

12 Getting to the top

Getting to the top 1

Charlotte Stone is the chief executive of British International Stores Group (BISG).

Charlotte Stone

Her father and mother **were** both factory workers.

She **was born** in Liverpool in 1955. She **went** to school there.

She **left school** at 16 and **joined** BISG. She **started work** in the BISG Liverpool shop as a **sales assistant**.

In 1988 she **became** head of the Liverpool shop.

In 1996 she **got a job** as **head of sales** for BISG. She **moved to** London.

In 2004 she became BISG chief executive.

Getting to the top 2

Mark South

– What **did** his parents **do**?
His father **was** a company director and his mother **worked** at a furniture company. She was in charge of designing the furniture.

– Where was he born?
He was born in London in 1956 and **went** to school there.

– When did he leave school?
In 1974 he left school and went to Oxford University.

– What did he **study** there?
He **studied** economics.

– What did he do next?
In 1977 he left Oxford University and went to Harvard for a year.

– Which company did he **join** after that?
In 1978 he joined Snares, a big company in New York with department stores all over the US.

– When did he **come back** to London?
He **came back** to London in 2003 and joined BISG as head of finance.

To learn more about the past simple, see page 109.

12.1 Complete the table. Look at A and B opposite to help you. Use the verb list on page 112 if you need more help.

Base form (infinitive)	Second form (past simple)
be	was/were
become	
	came
do	
get	
go	
	joined
leave	
move	
start	
	studied
work	

12.2 Complete the interview using verbs from 12.1 above. Look at A and B opposite to help you.

Interviewer: Where were you born?
Charlotte: I was born in Liverpool.

Interviewer: And where did you (1) .... to school?
Charlotte: I (2) .... to school there too.

Interviewer: What (3) .... your father and mother do?
Charlotte: They were both factory workers. They (4) .... in a car factory.

Interviewer: When did you leave school?
Charlotte: In 1971. I (5) .... BISG in that year.

Interviewer: When did you (6) .... head of the Liverpool store?
Charlotte: I (7) .... head in 1988.

Interviewer: And when did you (8) .... to London?
Charlotte: When I (9) .... the job as head of sales for BISG in 1996.

Interviewer: And when did you become chief executive of BISG?
Charlotte: I became chief executive in 2004.

Interviewer: How are things going?
Charlotte: Very well, thanks!

Over to you

Write down some key dates and events in your life and talk about them. Where did you go to school? What did you do next?

13 Skills

A Are you good with computers?

Charlotte is	**very good with** people. **good with** figures (= numbers).
She **isn't** (= is not) **very good with** computers.	

Mark **is**	**very good with** figures. **good with** computers.
He **isn't** (= is not) **very good with** people.	

B Skills

Charlotte is very good with people. She **has people skills.** She isn't very good with computers. She **doesn't** (= does not) **have** computer skills.

Mark is very good with computers. He **has computer skills.** He isn't very good with people. He **doesn't** (= does not) **have** people skills.

Charlotte also has very good
- **management skills** – she's a very good manager.
- **listening skills** – she listens carefully to what people say.
- **language skills** – she speaks very good Spanish.

Mark also has very good
- **problem-solving skills** – he finds an answer to every problem.
- **presentation skills** – he explains things very clearly.
- **negotiating skills** – he always gets the best price.

C Skilled and unskilled workers

At BISG, there are a lot of **skilled workers** – people with special skills – for example:

computer
programmers

store managers

There are also **unskilled** workers – without special skills – for example:

cleaners

warehouse workers

13.1 Write sentences to say what the people are good with. Look at A opposite to help you.

1 Boris likes computers and he knows how they work.

   He's good with computers.

2 When Jocasta uses a computer, she has problems.

....

3 When employees are unhappy, Jocasta can help them.

....

4 When employees are unhappy, Boris can't help them.

....

5 When Boris looks at the company's figures, he knows how to make them better.

....

6 When Jocasta looks at the company's figures, she understands them.

....

13.2 Now describe the skills of the people in 13.1 above. Look at B opposite to help you.

Boris has computer skills.

....

....

....

13.3 Answer the questions. What skills do employees in a company need to do the things below? Look at B opposite to help you.

1 Sell products to countries where people speak another language.

....

2 Find answers to problems.

....

3 Tell people clearly about their ideas and products.

....

4 Sell products at the right price, when the customers don't want to pay that price.

....

5 Understand what customers say.

....

6 Manage the company well.

....

Over to you

Are you good with:

☐ computers?　　☐ people?　　☐ figures?

14 | Qualifications and training

A ## Qualifications

Look at Mark South's **business card**.

BISG
290 Park Lane, London W1
Tel: +44 20 970 2000 **Fax:** +44 20 970 2055
Email: mark.south@bisg.co.uk

Mark South, BSc (Economics), MBA ⟵ qualifications
Finance Director ⟵ job title

BSc (Bachelor of Science) and BA (Bachelor of Arts) are types of **degree**, a qualification after a three- or four-year **course** at a university.

An MBA (Master of Business Administration) is a type of **Master's degree**, a higher qualification after another year at a university.

B ## Training

Training is for a job. For example, you can **train as** a doctor, an architect, an accountant, or an engineer.

You can **go on a training course** to **learn skills** in computers, management and other areas.

Charlotte Stone didn't go to university, but she had **on-the-job training** – she learnt how to do her job while she worked. And she has a lot of **experience** – she worked as a store manager for a long time and she knows the job well.

14.1 Complete the business card with the information below. Look at A opposite to help you.

Her name is Samantha Unwin.

She studied French for three years at university.

She is in charge of the training department.

BISG

290 Park Lane, London W1

Tel: +44 20 970 2000   **Fax:** +44 20 970 2055

Email: sam.unwin@bisg.co.uk

.... , ... (French)

....

14.2 Complete the interview. Look at B opposite to help you.

Interviewer: Melanie, how many buildings have you designed?
Melanie: Over thirty.
Interviewer: So you have a lot of (1) .... ! Do you use computers in your work?
Melanie: Yes, I do. But I trained (2) .... an architect in the 1970s, and computers weren't important then.
Interviewer: So what did you do to (3) .... computer (4) .... ?
Melanie: I learnt about the job while I worked: you know, (5) .... - .... - .... training.
Interviewer: Was that enough?
Melanie: No, it wasn't. So I decided to go on a three-month full-time (6) .... in 1990 to get these skills.

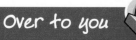

Over to you

Think of your job or one you would like. Are qualifications needed? Is training important?

15 Numbers and time

A Talking about the time

What's the time? (= What time is it?)

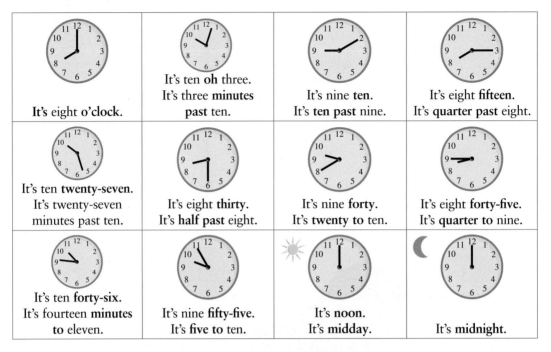

It's eight o'clock.	It's ten **oh** three. It's three **minutes past** ten.	It's nine **ten**. It's **ten past** nine.	It's eight **fifteen**. It's **quarter past** eight.
It's ten **twenty-seven**. It's twenty-seven minutes past ten.	It's eight **thirty**. It's **half past** eight.	It's nine **forty**. It's **twenty to** ten.	It's eight **forty-five**. It's **quarter to** nine.
It's ten **forty-six**. It's fourteen **minutes to** eleven.	It's nine **fifty-five**. It's **five to** ten.	It's **noon**. It's **midday**.	It's **midnight**.

> BrE/AmE: twenty–five past eight; AmE: twenty–five after eight
> BrE/AmE: twenty to nine; AmE: twenty of nine

B Start and finish times

You can talk about start and finish times like this:

> The bank opens **at** nine thirty and it closes **at** five.

> I work **from** nine **to** five.

> In the UK, banks are open **from** half past nine **until** half past three.

C Morning, afternoon, evening and night

The bank opens at	nine thirty half past nine	in the morning.
	9.30 **am**.	

The bank closes at	four thirty half past four	in the afternoon.
	4.30 **pm**.	

The bar opens at	nine nine o'clock	in the evening.
	9.00 **pm**.	

The bank is closed **at night**.

15.1 Complete the sentences using words only. Look at A opposite to help you.

1

It's ....
It's ....

3

It's ....
It's ....

5

It's ....
It's ....

2

It's ....

4

It's ....
It's ....

6

It's ....
It's ....

15.2 Complete the sentences using the information on the signs. Look at B and C opposite to help you.

1 **Shop opening hours 10.30 am to 4.00 pm**

The shop is open .... ten thirty ....
.... to four ....
....

2 **Barry's Place 10 pm to 3 am**

The night club opens .... ten ....
.... and closes .... three
....

3 **Syd's supermarket** *Monday – Saturday* *8.00 – 6.00*

The supermarket opens .... eight ....
.... and closes at six ....
....

4 **National Bank of Restoria** Monday – Friday 8.30 – 12.45

The bank opens .... eight thirty ....
.... and closes .... quarter to
one. It doesn't open again ....
.... !

Over to you

What time is it now? What time do you go to work? What time do you get home?

16 Timetables

A Timetables

This is the **twenty-four-hour clock**.

seventeen **hundred** (hours)

twenty-three **hundred** (hours)

oh nine thirty (hours)

ten **oh** five

twenty-one **twenty** (hours)

twenty-three **fifty-nine**

It is used mainly for **timetables** (= information about times of trains, planes, etc.).

BrE: timetable; AmE: schedule

B Talking about travel times

Look at this **train timetable**.

Leaves London Paddington	20.15
Arrives in Reading	20.30
Leaves Reading	20.35
Arrives in Swindon	21.15
Leaves Swindon	21.19
Arrives in Bath	21.40
Leaves Bath	21.43
Arrives in Bristol	22.00

When What time	does	the train it	leave arrive in	Paddington? Bristol?

It The train	leaves leaves Paddington	at	twenty fifteen. 8.15 pm.
It The train	arrives arrives in Bristol		twenty-two hundred (hours). 10 pm.

How long	does	the journey it	take	from Paddington to Bristol?

It takes	one hour (and) forty-five minutes. an hour and three-quarters.

It's a **direct** train. You don't **change** trains.

16.1 Complete the times on the clocks using the 24-hour clock. Look at A opposite to help you.

1 oh six thirty   **3** eighteen fourteen   **5** twenty-one twelve

2 sixteen forty-five   **4** twenty hundred   **6** twenty-three eleven

16.2 Complete the questions and answers about the timetable below. Look at A and B opposite to help you.

Train 1

Leaves Singapore	08.30
Arrives in Kuala Lumpur	15.00

Train 2

Leaves Kuala Lumpur	20.10
Arrives in Butterworth	06.10 the next day

Train 3

Leaves Butterworth	14.30
Arrives in Bangkok	10.00 the next day

1 A: When does the train leave Singapore?
   B: It .... Singapore .... 08.30.
2 A: Is it a .... train?
   B: No, it isn't. You .... trains in Kuala Lumpur and Butterworth.
3 A: When does the train arrive in Kuala Lumpur?
   B: It .... Kuala Lumpur ....
4 A: .... time .... it .... Kuala Lumpur?
   B: It leaves Kuala Lumpur at 20.10.
5 A: .... it .... in Butterworth?
   B: It arrives in Butterworth .... the next day.
6 A: .... Butterworth?
   B: It leaves Butterworth ....
7 A: When .... Bangkok?
   B: .... Bangkok .... 10.00 the next day.

16.3 Ask and answer questions about these journeys using the timetable in 16.2 above.
Look at B opposite to help you.

1 Singapore – Bangkok
2 Singapore – Kuala Lumpur
3 Kuala Lumpur – Butterworth
4 Butterworth – Bangkok

1 A: How long does the journey take from Singapore to Bangkok?
   B: It takes twenty-five and a half hours.

 Over to you

Write five questions and answers about a journey that you know.

17 Days and dates

A Months and seasons

January	February	March	April	May	June
July	August	September	October	November	December

> The New Year begins **in January**.

spring summer autumn winter

> I take three weeks' holiday **in summer**.

BrE: autumn; AmE: fall

B Days and dates

		You say …	You write …
1st	first	**the** first **of** August, August **the** first	1 August, 1st August, August 1st
2nd	second	the second of August, August the second	2 August, 2nd August, August 2nd
3rd	third	the third of August, August the third	3 August, 3rd August, August 3rd
4th	fourth	the fourth of August, August the fourth	4 August, 4th August, August 4th
5th	fifth	the fifth of August, August the fifth	5 August, 5th August, August 5th

AmE: You usually say 'August first' and you always write 'August 1' or 'August 1st'
BrE: 1/8 in informal writing; AmE: 8/1

Look at this **calendar**.

						AUGUST
Monday	**Tuesday**	**Wednesday**	**Thursday**	**Friday**	**Saturday**	**Sunday**
	1	2	3	4	5	6
7	8	9	10	11	12	13
14	15	16	17	18	19	20
21	22	23	24	25	26	27
28	29	30	31			

Be careful with:

20th	twentieth	22nd	twenty-second	30th	thirtieth
21st	twenty-first	23rd	twenty-third	31st	thirty-first

Monday to Friday are **weekdays** and Saturday and Sunday are the **weekend**.

> The training course starts on the twenty-third of February.

> The meeting is on Monday the seventh of June.

C Public holidays

Some days are **national holidays** or **public holidays** when many businesses are closed.
For example:

New Year's Day is **on** January 1st.   May 1st is a national holiday in many countries.

BrE: public holidays are also called bank holidays

17.1 Write each date in one of the ways you can *say* it. Look at A and B opposite to help you.

1 17 Mar (St Patrick's Day, Ireland)
the seventeenth of March OR March the seventeenth OR March seventeenth

2 25 Apr (Anzac Day, Australia and New Zealand)

3 4 Jul (Independence Day, US)

4 14 Jul (Bastille Day, France)

5 29 Oct (Republic Day, Turkey)

6 20 Nov (Revolution Day, Mexico)

7 31 Dec (New Year's Eve)

17.2 Write the days and dates of the shows, using the calendar and the information about an exhibition centre. Look at B opposite to help you.

March					April	
SUN	MON	TUE	WED	THU	FRI	SAT
27	28	29	30	31	1	2
3	4	5	6	7	8	9
10	11	12	13	14	15	16
17	18	19	20	21	22	23

SPRING AT THE SHOW CENTRE

1 Cat Show   28/3
2 Business Show   31/3
3 Fashion Show   2/4
4 Home Show   3/4
5 Boat Show   20/4

1 The Cat Show is on Monday 28th March.

2

3

4

5

17.3 Complete the sentences. Look at A, B and C opposite to help you.

1 Her birthday is .... June.
2 Earth Day is .... 22nd April.
3 The office is too hot .... summer and too cold .... winter.
4 I usually go on holiday .... August.
5 The main national holiday in France is .... July 14th.

Over to you

Write down the spoken and written forms of three dates that are important for you.

18 Time expressions

A Early or late?

I arrived at the meeting I was	early (= before the start time). half an hour early. 30 minutes early. on time (= just before or at the start time). late (= after the start time). three quarters of an hour late. 45 minutes late.

B Word combinations with 'time'

spend		= use time in a particular way
lose	time	= use more time for something than you planned
waste		= use time in a way that is not useful
save		= use less time for something than you planned

I usually **spend 30 minutes** every morning checking my email.

I **wasted two weeks** waiting for a reply to my letter.

We **saved two hours** by getting a direct flight to Hong Kong.

C Adverbs of frequency

always	✓✓✓✓✓✓✓
usually	✓✓✓✓✓
often	✓✓✓
sometimes	✓
never	✗

I	always usually often sometimes never	get to work late.

A: **How often** do you arrive at work on time?
B: I **usually** arrive at work on time.

18.1 Complete the sentences. Look at the times that these things usually start, and the times that they started last week. Look at A opposite to help you.

	Normal time	Time last week
Sales meeting 1 Last week it started ....20...... minutes ...late.... .	Monday 9.00 am	Monday 9.20 am
Presentation by the boss to all employees 2 Last week it started	Tuesday 10.30 am	Tuesday 10.30 am
Open-day presentation for visitors 3 Last week it started	Wednesday 2.15 pm	Wednesday 2.45 pm
Conference call with the New York office 4 Last week it started	Thursday 4.00 pm	Thursday 4.10 pm
Drink at the pub 5 Last week it started	Friday 5.00 pm	Friday 4.30 pm

18.2 Match the two parts of the sentences. Look at B opposite to help you.

1 I lost time when my
2 They wasted three days in London
3 We saved a lot of time
4 She spent a lot of time planning –

a because the office was closed for holidays.
b it was a good presentation!
c computer crashed.
d after we bought faster computers.

18.3 Write sentences with adverbs to say how often you do the things below. Use each adverb once only. Look at C opposite to help you.

How often do you:
1 go to the theatre in the evening? ✓

    I sometimes go to the theatre in the evening.
2 have lunch at a restaurant? ✓✓✓✓

    ....
3 go skiing in winter? ✗

    ....
4 watch television in the evening? ✓✓✓✓✓✓

    ....
5 go to the gym? ✓✓✓

    ....

Over to you

Talk about what you do in a week, as in 18.3 above, using the adverbs in this unit.

19 Do you have time?

A I don't have time

Look at this **diary**.

May	Mon 11	Tues 12	Weds 13	Thurs 14	Fri 15
am	10.00 Sales meeting	9.15 Meet customer	10.15 Meet customer		9.30 See (= meet) manager
pm	2.30 Appointment with dentist	2.00 Work at the office	2.00 Work on customer orders		

Can we meet on Monday?

No, I'm afraid I **don't have time** to meet on Monday. I'm **busy**. **I'm going to** a sales meeting in the morning and **I have an appointment with** my dentist in the afternoon.

What are you doing on Friday?

I'm	going to a sales meeting meeting a customer working at the office seeing my manager having lunch with a customer	(on Friday).

B Are you free on Friday?

Are you free on Friday?

Yes, **I'm free on** Friday afternoon. **Where shall we meet?**

Let's meet	at	my/your office. a restaurant for lunch. a café for a coffee. a bar for a drink.

When shall we meet?

How What	about	12.30? one o'clock? 3.15? after work?

To learn more about the present continuous for future plans, see page 108.

19.1 Complete what Trevor says about each day next week, using his diary. Look at A and B opposite to help you.

September

Mon 22	Tues 23	Weds 24	Thurs 25	Fri 26
10.00 am Go to a sales meeting	9.15 am Visit a customer	9.00 am Work at the office	8.00 am See my manager	9.45 am Visit Mr Smith
2.00 pm Work on sales plans	2.00 pm Meet my daughter's teacher at her school	2.30 pm Visit Altex Ltd	1.45 pm Appointment with the doctor Then go back to office	2.00 pm Play golf with Mr Smith 5.00 pm free

1 On Monday I'm <u>going to a sales meeting in the morning. I'm working on sales plans in</u>
<u>the afternoon</u> .

2 On Tuesday I'm ....

3 On Wednesday I'm ....
....

4 On Thursday I'm ....
....

5 On Friday I'm ....
....

19.2 Complete the conversation. Look at B opposite to help you.

Damien: Are you free for a coffee on Tuesday afternoon?
Emily: I'm afraid I'm (1) .... on Tuesday afternoon. I'm seeing a customer.
Damien: Can we (2) .... on Wednesday?
Emily: Yes, I'm (3) .... on Wednesday.
Damien: Where (4) .... we meet?
Emily: Let's meet (5) .... Luigi's café.
Damien: (6) .... shall we meet?
Emily: (7) .... about four o'clock?
Damien: See you there at four!

Over to you

Look at your diary. What are you doing each day next week?

20 Free time and holidays

A Free time

What do you do in your free time (= when you are not working)?

Do you play an instrument?

What about you? How do you **relax** (= rest after working)?

I'm going swimming on Friday. Are you free then?

I go swimming at the pool near my office and **I play a lot of** golf. I play **at least twice a week** (= two times a week or more).

I'm interested in music, so I go to a concert **once a week** (= one time every week).

Yes, in my free time, **I play the** piano, but not very often!

Yes, I can **take a break** (= stop work for a short time) in the afternoon.

B Word combinations with 'have' and 'take'

have take	**a break** **a coffee break / a tea break** **your lunch break**
	a day off / the day off **a week off / the week off**
	a long weekend (= take a day off on Friday or Monday to add to the weekend)
	a holiday three **days' holiday** two **weeks' holiday**

Note: 'a day off' or 'a week off' can be a holiday or for illness
'have' = the company gives you the time; 'take' = you decide to take the time

C Going on holiday

I **have** five **weeks' holiday** a year. I **take** three weeks in summer and two weeks in winter. And I sometimes **take long weekends** too!

In summer, I don't stay in France. I **go abroad** (= go to another country). I like to **go on holiday** somewhere very hot!

In winter, I stay in France. I **go skiing** in the Alps. Sometimes it's important to **take it easy** (= relax).

BrE: holiday; AmE: vacation

20.1 Complete the sentences with words from the box. Look at A and C opposite to help you.

music	walking	the piano	golf
the violin	reading	swimming	football

guitar

I go
- running.
- mountain climbing.
- ....
- ....

I like
I'm interested in
- modern art.
- history.
- ....
- ....

saxophone

I play
- the guitar.
- the saxophone.
- ....
- ....

I play
- rugby.
- tennis.
- ....
- ....

rugby

20.2 Complete the crossword. Look at A, B and C opposite to help you.

Across

1 I ....
tennis: I play every day. (4,1,3,2)

5 They .... at the pool near
their office every lunchtime. (2,8)

6 If you feel ill, ...
.... (4,3,3,3)

9 One time. (4)

11 Stop work to drink coffee. (4,1,6,5)

12 British English for 'vacation' (7)

13 Relax and take it .... ! (4)

14 Taking Friday off makes a long .... (7)

Down

2 I don't go on holiday in my own country:
I go .... (6)

3 Two times. (5)

4 A: Are you .... in the local football
team? B: Yes, I go to every match. (10)

7 When you're not working it's your
.... (4,4)

8 Don't work too hard. You must ....
sometimes! (5)

10 Dan goes .... in the Dolomites
every winter. (6)

Over to you

How do you relax?

21 Numbers and money

A Amounts of money 1

You talk about **exact** (= complete) amounts of money like this:

$12.99	twelve dollars (and) ninety-nine cents twelve dollars ninety-nine twelve ninety-nine
£211.53	two hundred and eleven pounds (and) fifty-three pence two hundred and eleven pounds fifty-three two hundred and eleven fifty-three
€33,972.35	thirty-three thousand nine hundred and seventy-two euros (and) thirty-five cents thirty-three thousand nine hundred and seventy two euros thirty-five thirty-three thousand nine hundred and seventy two, thirty-five

When you write amounts of money on a **cheque** (= printed form from the bank), you give as much information as possible:

$12.99	twelve dollars (and) ninety-nine cents
£211.53	two hundred and eleven pounds (and) fifty-three pence
€33,972.35	thirty-three thousand nine hundred and seventy-two euros (and) thirty-five cents

> BrE: cheque; AmE: check
> BrE: You usually say 'and' in figures; AmE: You don't usually say 'and'

To learn more about 'and' in figures, see Unit 4.

B Amounts of money 2

You talk about large amounts of money like this:

£2,250,000	**two and a quarter** million pounds
€6,500,000,000	**six and a half** billion euros
¥19,750,000,000	**nineteen and three quarter** billion yen

To learn more about fractions, see Unit 5.

C Approximate amounts

When you want to give an idea of the size of the figure, you use 'of':

This camera **costs**	hundreds thousands millions billions	of	pounds. euros. dollars. yen.

You can also use words to show that the figure is not exact – it is near this amount, but may be higher or lower.

The price of this house **is**	about around roughly approximately	£2,500,000.

When you give an **exact figure** (= complete amount), you do not use the word 'of'. For example, you say:

This camera costs **five hundred and twenty-five euros**.

Note: 'Approximately' is more formal than 'about', 'around' and 'roughly'.

21.1 Complete the cheques. Look at A opposite to help you.

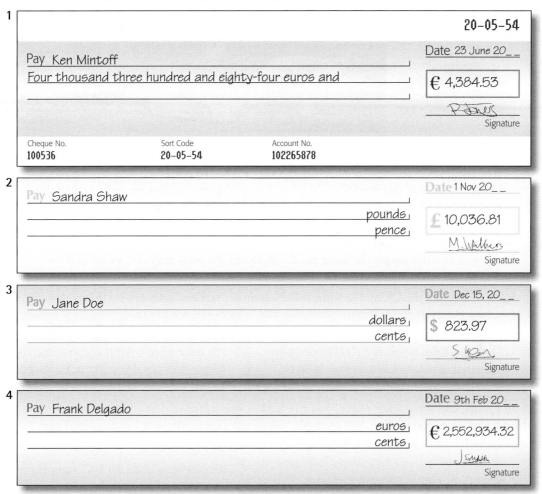

1

20-05-54

Pay Ken Mintoff

Four thousand three hundred and eighty-four euros and

Date 23 June 20_ _

€ 4,384.53

Signature

Cheque No.
100536

Sort Code
20-05-54

Account No.
102265878

2

Pay Sandra Shaw

pounds

pence

Date 1 Nov 20_ _

£ 10,036.81

Signature

3

Pay Jane Doe

dollars

cents

Date Dec 15, 20_ _

$ 823.97

Signature

4

Pay Frank Delgado

euros

cents

Date 9th Feb 20_ _

€ 2,552,934.32

Signature

21.2 Write and talk about these prices without giving an exact figure. Look at C opposite to help you.

1 €599   hundreds of euros
2 $86,666
3 £2.7 billion
4 €40,000,000

21.3 Use approximate figures to write and talk about these houses and flats using the words in brackets ( ). Look at C opposite to help you.

1 chateau, €9,950,000 (about) The price of the chateau is about ten million euros.

2 villa, €705,000 (around) ....

3 flat, €299,500 (roughly) ....

4 studio, €50,500 (approximately) ....

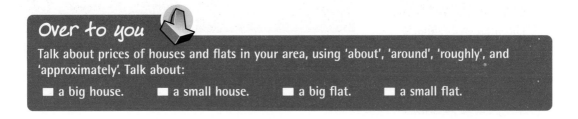

Over to you

Talk about prices of houses and flats in your area, using 'about', 'around', 'roughly', and 'approximately'. Talk about:

■ a big house.   ■ a small house.   ■ a big flat.   ■ a small flat.

22 Prices

A Talking about prices

| £19,995 | £24,950 | £39,000 | £48,700 |

| **How much is** the red one?
 What's the price of this model?
 How much does the X-type **cost**? | The red one **is**
 The price of this model is
 The X-type **costs** | £19,995. |

B Tax

Sometimes you **pay tax on** the **basic price** – this gives the **total price**. Prices are shown **including tax** or **excluding tax**.

In some states in the US, and in some other countries, you pay **sales tax** on things that you buy. For example, in Pennsylvania, the **rate** of sales tax is 6 per cent.

> This beautiful book is $100.00 per copy.
> Pennsylvania residents **add** sales tax of $6.00.

> The basic price is $100 and you add six dollars sales tax if you live in Pennsylvania.

In Europe and some other places, you pay **VAT** (**value added tax**) **at** a particular **rate** on some products and services. For example, the rate in France for most things is 19.5 per cent, and in the UK it's 17.5 per cent.

> Mountain Castle computer game
> £20.00 excl. VAT, £23.50 inc. VAT at 17.5 per cent.

> We have to add £3.50 VAT onto the basic price of £20, so the price including VAT is £23.50.

Note: inc. or incl. = including; excl. = excluding
These are **abbreviations** (= short ways of writing something).

C 'Value' and 'worth'

If you want to talk about the price of something which is not for sale, you can use '**value**' or '**worth**'.

The value of Cézanne's 'Auvers-sur-Oise' is €10 million.

The Hope diamond **is worth** $250 million.

These Fabergé eggs **are worth** €500,000 each.

22.1 Complete the conversation about the DVD players. Look at A opposite to help you.

A: (1) .... is this one?
B: This one (2) .... $50.
A: And what's the (3) ....
that one over there?
B: That one is $30.
A: And what about the black one? How
(4) .... that one (5) .... ?
B: That one (6) .... $20.

22.2 True or false? Look at B opposite to help you.

1 The basic price is the same as the price including tax.
2 VAT stands for 'value added tax'.
3 The abbreviation for 'excluding' is 'excl.'.
4 People in the US pay VAT.
5 People pay sales tax in all states of the US.

22.3 Complete the sentences. Look at C opposite to help you.

1 The value .... this house .... $37 million.

2 These bottles of perfume .... worth £50,000 each.

3 The value of .... sculpture .... $5,600,000.

4 These planes .... worth $187 million each.

5 This painting .... worth €100 million.

6 The value .... this shopping centre ....
$2 billion.

Over to you

Is there sales tax or VAT in your country? If so, what are the rates for different types of products? How much is the tax on food and books?

23 Notes and coins

Currency

The money used in a country is its **currency**.

The currency in Australia is the Australian dollar (A$). There are **notes** or **banknotes** for:

A$100   A$50   A$20   A$10   A$5

The Australian dollar is **divided into** 100 cents (¢). There are **coins** for:

A$2   A$1   50¢   20¢   10¢   5¢

a hundred-dollar note

a fifty-cent coin

> BrE: note, banknote;
> AmE: bill

B Changing money

Marion is going on holiday to Australia. To **change** or **exchange money,** she goes to a **bank** or a **bureau de change.** She asks these questions:

a   What's the currency in Australia?

b   What's the **exchange rate**? **How many** Australian dollars **are there to** the euro?

c   Do you sell **traveller's cheques**? Are they easy **to cash** in Australia?

d   How much **commission** do you charge? (= How much does it cost to change money)?

e   If I have some Australian currency at the end of my holiday, can I **change it back** into euros?

> BrE: traveller's cheque;
> AmE: traveler's check

23.1 Match the notes and coins of Doradia (1–6) to their names (a–f). Look at A opposite to help you.

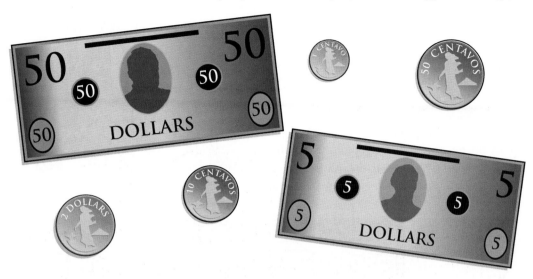

a a two-dollar coin
b a fifty-dollar note
c a five-dollar note
d a fifty-centavo coin
e a ten-centavo coin
f a one-centavo coin

23.2 Complete the sentences using information from 23.1 above. Look at A opposite to help you.

A: How was your holiday in Doradia?
B: Great, thanks. I'm just going to the bank to (1) .... the money I
   didn't spend.
A: What's the (2) .... in Doradia?
B: It's the Doradian dollar. This is a (3) ....-..................... ....
A: Oh, it's very colourful!
B: Yes. Did you know that the Doradian dollar is (4) .... one hundred
   centavos? Look, this is a fifty-centavo (5) .... This is ten centavos, and these smaller
   ones are one centavo.

23.3 Match the answers below to the questions in B opposite.

1 There are 1.6 Australian dollars to the euro.
2 We charge one per cent commission on banknotes, but for traveller's cheques, we charge two
  per cent commission.
3 It's the Australian dollar.
4 Yes, you can change the notes back, but not the coins.
5 Yes, we sell traveller's cheques in euros and US dollars. Banks, hotels and restaurants will cash
  them – no problem.

Over to you

Talk about the notes and coins of a country that you have visited recently. What is the
exchange rate?

24 Can I afford it?

A It's so expensive

Kim works as a teacher in London.

'Living in the city is very **expensive**! Transport and clothes **cost a lot** of money and food **prices** are **high** too.

I **can't afford** to go out very often: I don't have enough money. I **spend** all my money. I don't have any money left at the end of the month – it's difficult to **save** (= keep and not spend).'

B Careful with money

Kim is talking with a friend, Lisa.

Lisa: Are you **careful with money**?
Kim: Yes, I am. I try not to spend too much.
Lisa: How do you try to **save money**?
Kim: I try not to spend too much. I go to shops when there is a **sale** – with lower prices than usual.
Lisa: Yes, when I'm at the supermarket, I look for **special offers** – for example when you get two products for the price of one.
Kim: And I try not to **waste money** by buying things I don't need.

C Loans

Lisa: Are you **renting** (= paying money to live in a building that someone else owns) or buying your house?
Kim: I'm buying it. I **borrowed** £200,000 from the bank but it's difficult to **repay** the **loan**. What about you?
Lisa: The bank **lent** me £185,000 and I have to **pay back** £700 per month.

Note: You can say '£700 **per** month' or '£700 **a** month'.

24.1 Complete the table. Look at A, B and C opposite to help you. Use the verb list on page 00 if you need more help.

Verb base form (infinitive)	Noun
	cost
lend	
	repayment
	savings

24.2 Choose the correct word to complete each sentence. Look at A, B and C opposite to help you.

1 The bank .... (lent/loan) me £150,000 and I .... (repay/repayment) £550 a month.
2 I have a .... (loan/lend) to buy a car. The .... (repayments/repaid) for this are £90 per month.
3 It .... (cost/costs) so much to eat out in restaurants! I prefer to eat at home.
4 I get £2,000 a month from my job. I spend £1,800 and .... (save/savings) £200.
5 I .... (borrow/borrowed) £10,000 for a long holiday. Then I won some money so I .... (repay/repaid) £5,000.

24.3 Complete the sentences. Look at A, B and C opposite to help you.

1 If you want to buy things at lower prices, you go to a shop where there's a ....
2 If you want to buy things more cheaply at supermarkets, you look for ....
3 If you don't have enough money to buy something, you .... it.
4 If you spend more money than necessary, you .... money.
5 If something costs a lot of money, it is ....
6 If you pay money to live in a house or flat owned by someone else, you .... it.

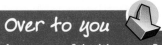
Over to you

Are you careful with money? What do you do to save money? Is it easy?

A Wages

staff: the people who work for a company

Superfastfood Restaurants

We are looking for **staff** for our restaurants.

35-hour week

Wages: Earn €5 per hour **basic pay**

€6 per hour **overtime**

Free meals: all the hamburgers you can eat!

Email personal details to
recruitment@superfastfood.com

basic pay: money you get for working the normal hours each week (35 hours in this job)

wages: the money you get if you are paid every week

earn: get

overtime: money you get for working more than your normal hours

B Salaries

Orbit Business Television – Producers

We are looking for producers at our studios in Frankfurt.

Salary: €90,000 per year

Working hours: Monday to Friday, 9.00 am – 5.30 pm

Benefits
– 30 days' **holiday** per year
– **Company restaurant** with cheap meals
– **Company car**
– **Company pension**
Email humanresources@orbitbusinesstv.de

salary: the money you get if you are paid every month

benefits: the things you get in addition to money

pension: money you get after you stop working, for example at 60 or 65 years old

BrE: holiday;
AmE: vacation

25.1 Match the two parts of the word combinations. Look at A and B opposite to help you.

1 basic	a hours
2 company	b meals
3 company	c pay
4 free	d pension
5 working	e car

25.2 Complete the sentences using word combinations from 25.1 above. Look at A and B opposite to help you.

1 It's great – I can sell my own car. They're giving me a
....

2 They offer a .... for when I get old.

3 I get .... ,
but I don't like hamburgers!

4 The ....
are very long: I finish work
very late.

5 The .... is
very bad, but the overtime
is good.

25.3 Match the two parts of the sentences. Look at A and B opposite to help you.

1 I'm looking for a job with a better salary:	a you have to pay €2 for lunch.
2 The company restaurant isn't free:	b but I can always work overtime.
3 It's a 25-hour week,	c I don't earn enough where I am now.
4 The other staff are very friendly:	d that's six weeks a year.
5 I get 30 days' holiday:	e I have a company car.
6 The benefits are excellent:	f I like everyone working there.

Over to you

Write an advertisement for your dream job using expressions from this unit.

26 Banks

Accounts

Kim is the teacher we met in Unit 24.

'I'm **with** ADKL **Bank**. I have a **cheque account** with a **cheque book** so I can **write cheques** (= printed forms from the bank). My salary is **paid directly into** my account. I also have a **savings account** where I save money and **earn interest** (= money the bank pays you).

I can **transfer money** between these two accounts – I can move money from one account into the other. I can go to the bank to do this, but it's easier to use ADKL's **internet banking** service.

The bank send me a **statement** (= a printed list of payments from and to the account) every month, showing me the **balance** (= how much money I have in the account).'

> BrE: cheque; AmE: check
> BrE: cheque account, **current account**;
> AmE: checking account

Cards

Lisa: Do you have a **cash card**?

Kim: Yes, I use it to **take out** or **withdraw** money from **cash machines**. I can use the money to **pay cash** for things in shops.

Lisa: And do you have a **credit card** like Visa or American Express?

Kim: Yes, I do. It has a **limit** of £5,000 – that's the maximum amount I can spend – but I try to repay what I **owe** (= need to pay back) every month. I don't want to **get into debt** and owe a lot of money without being able to repay it.

Lisa: I know the problem!

Note: Cash machines are also called **ATMs** (automatic teller machines), especially in the US.

26.1 Complete the crossword. Look at A and B opposite to help you.

Across

2 If you have a job, you .... money for the work that you do. (4)

3 When you can look at your account on computer: internet .... (7)

5 You can make payments from this. (6,7)

7 You can get cash from this. (4,7)

9 If you don't spend money, you .... it. (4)

12 Another name for an account with a chequebook. (7)

13 Another expression for 'withdraw'. (4,3)

15 If you spend more money than you have, you .... (3,4,4)

17 and 19 across and 6 down My salary is .... into my .... (4,8,7)

Down

1 What you use to get money at 7 across. (4,4)

4 Extra money that you get when you save. (8)

8 Mastercard is a type of .... (6,4)

10 'Complete' a cheque: .... it. (5)

11 Another expression for 'take out'. (8)

12 You can use one instead of cash to pay for something. (6)

14 A place where you can get money when the bank is closed. (1,1,1)

16 To move money from one account to another is to .... it. (7)

18 If you have an account at a bank, you are .... that bank. (4)

26.2 Complete the text with words from the box. Look at B opposite to help you.

take out	owed	debt	limit
credit card	cash machine	cash card	

Jon got his first (1) .... when he was a student. At that time it had a (2) .... of €3,000. When he got his first job, the bank raised the limit to €10,000. Jon spent too much and got into (3) .... He couldn't pay what he (4) .... every month. In the end, he paid back the debt, but he doesn't want another credit card.

Jane withdrew money one day at a (5) .... with her (6) .... Later she looked in her handbag and her card had gone – someone had stolen it. She remembered someone was looking over her shoulder when she was at the cash machine. They used it to (7) .... all the cash in her cheque account.

 Over to you

When you pay for different things, how do you pay?

27 Product details

A Dimensions

A journalist is talking to the marketing manager of Samson, a mobile phone company. The product is **coming out** (= Samson is selling it for the first time) next month.

Journalist:	What is the Samson 500? What does it do?
Marketing manager:	It's a mobile phone and it's also a small computer.
Journalist:	**What are its dimensions?**
Marketing manager:	**It's** 10 centimetres **by** 10 centimetres, and 1 centimetre **thick**.
Journalist:	That's an interesting **shape**!
Marketing manager:	Yes, it's not **rectangular**. It's **square**.
Journalist:	**How big is** the **screen**?
Marketing manager:	The screen is 5 centimetres **wide** by 7 centimetres **long**.
Journalist:	**How much does it weigh?**
Marketing manager:	It's not **heavy** – it's very **light**. **It weighs** only 120 grams.

✗ ✓

> BrE: millimetre, centimetre, metre;
> AmE: millimeter, centimeter, meter

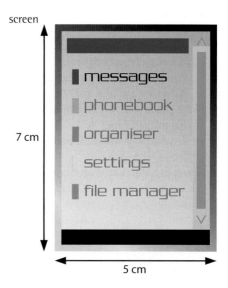

screen

10 cm

7 cm

1 cm

10 cm

5 cm

B Features

The journalist asks about the **features** (= important points) of the Samson 500.

Journalist:	**How fast** is the computer in the Samson 500?
Marketing manager:	It's very **fast**. It works **at** very **high speeds**.
Journalist:	**What does it do?**
Marketing manager:	It stores names and addresses, you can write notes on it and it has a clock with an alarm.
Journalist:	Is it **easy to use**?
Marketing manager:	Yes, very easy. You don't need to read the book that comes with it!

27.1 Complete the tables. Look at A and B opposite to help you.

Adjective	Noun
long	length
	width
	thickness
	square
	rectangle

Verb	Noun
	weight

27.2 Complete the sentences using words from 27.1 above.
Look at A opposite to help you.

1 The screen is 105 centimetres .... The ....
of the screen is 105 centimetres.
2 Its .... is 4 centimetres. It's 4 centimetres ....
3 It's not square. It's ....
4 It .... 20 kilograms.

4 cm

105 cm

27.3 Complete the sentences. Look at B opposite to help you.

1

Oh no! I paid €100 for this, but ....
.... do?

2

Everything is clear. I understand! It's very ....
.... !

3

This computer isn't very .... It takes a long time just
to send an email!

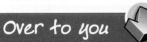

Over to you

Talk about a product that you use, using expressions from this unit.

28 Service companies

A A service company

Sid's Taxi Services
0800 833 8222
Any time – any distance
Our drivers are
friendly   reliable   helpful
Our cars are
clean   comfortable
Our fares are
LOW!

friendly

clean

low

reliable: they arrive at the right time

helpful: they help you with your bags

comfortable

B Talking about services

Joe is asking Tom about a conference hotel he visited last month.

What	was	the hotel the service the food	like?
	were	the hotel rooms	

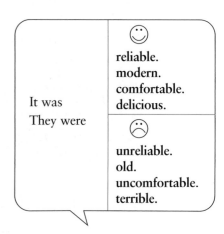

It was They were	☺ reliable. modern. comfortable. delicious.
	☹ unreliable. old. uncomfortable. terrible.

28.1 Complete the table. Look at A and B opposite to help you.

Adjective	Opposite
friendly	unfriendly
	unreliable
	unhelpful
	uncomfortable

clean	dirty
	high

28.2 Complete the conversation using adjectives from 28.1 above.

Anthea: Have you tried Tim's Taxi Services?
Belinda: Yes, and they're terrible! The drivers don't say 'hello' – they're so (1) ....
Anthea: Do the drivers arrive when you ask them to?
Belinda: No, they're always late – they're really (2) ....
Anthea: Do they carry your bags?
Belinda: No, they just sit in the car – they're so (3) ....
Anthea: And what about the cars? Are they clean?
Belinda: They never clean the taxis – they're always (4) ....
Anthea: And are the cars comfortable?
Belinda: No, they use very small cars, so you always feel (5) .... , and very tired at the end of the journey.
Anthea: And what about the fares?
Belinda: They're so (6) .... ! You pay so much! Try Sid's Taxi Services instead!

28.3 Complete the text about a conference hotel. Look at B opposite to help you.

The hotel was very (1) .... [☺], but the food was
(2) .... [☹].
The hotel rooms were very (3) .... [☺], but the service was
(4) .... [☹].

Over to you

Talk about a service that you use, using adjectives from this unit.

29 Where's it made?

A Manufactured products

Look at this Samson 3000 DVD player. **Where's it made?** (= Where is it made?)

It is It's They **are** They're	**made** **manufactured**	**in a**	**factory** **plant**	in China.

It's **shipped** to the United States.

It's **stored** in a warehouse.

It's **distributed** to a **retailer**: usually an **electrical goods shop**.

To learn more about the passive, see page 110.

B Food products

These vegetables are **grown** in East Africa. They are **picked** by hand.

They are **loaded** on planes the same day and they are **flown** to Europe.

They are **unloaded** and stored in warehouses, but only for a short time.

They are **sold** in **supermarkets** two days after they are picked. They are **bought** by **customers** in Europe and North America.

29.1 Complete the table. Look at A and B opposite to help you. Use the verb list on page 00 if you need more help.

Base form (infinitive)	Third form (past participle)
buy	
distribute	
fly	
grow	
load	
make	
manufacture	
sell	
ship	
store	
unload	

29.2 Complete the sentences. Look at A and B opposite to help you.

1 These clothes .... (make) in Vietnam.

2 For example, this type of T-shirt .... (manufacture) in a factory in Hanoi.

3 The T-shirts .... (load) into a container.

4 The container .... (ship) across the Pacific.

5 The container .... (unload) in San Francisco.

6 The T-shirts .... (store) in a warehouse.

7 They .... (distribute) by truck to the stores.

8 The T-shirts .... (sell) in stores all over North America.

 Over to you

Where are your favourite clothes made? Where do you buy them? How are they transported there?

Where's it sold?

A Shops and stores

trolley

checkout

You can buy food, clothes and sometimes other products in a **supermarket**. You can **use a trolley** and you **pay at a checkout** or **till**.

A **convenience store** is a small shop that is open from very early to very late. In the UK, a **corner shop** is a convenience store near your home, on the corner of two streets.

A **chain store** is one of a number of shops with the same name. These shops are all part of a **chain** (= group of stores owned by one company).

A **department store** is a large shop usually in a city centre. It sells many types of goods in **departments** or **sections** – for example clothes and furniture – on several **floors**.

A **mall** or **shopping mall** is a large building outside a town with many shops and a big car park.

> BrE: shop; AmE: store
> BrE: shopping trolley;
> AmE: shopping cart

B Direct sales

Some manufacturers use **direct sales** – selling to the customer without using a shop.

You can buy things **by mail order**. You **choose from a catalogue** and **order by post** or **on the phone**.

With **internet shopping** you buy things **over the internet** using the seller's **website**. Buying and selling like this is also called **e-commerce**.

> BrE: catalogue;
> AmE: catalog

30.1 Complete the crossword. Look at A and B opposite to help you.

Across

2 A book where you choose what to buy. (9)

3 Buying without going to a shop. (6,5)

7 You buy food and some other things in a .... (11)

9 Where you buy things when other shops are closed. (11,5)

11 When you buy things by post: mail .... (5)

12 and 13 A building with a lot of shops. (8,4)

14 The place where you pay in a supermarket. (8)

Down

1 On the internet, you buy things on a company's .... (7)

5 Buying and selling things on the internet. (1–8)

6 In the UK, a shop near your home which is open late. (6,4)

8 In this type of large shop, there are lots of different .... (11)

10 British English for shopping 'cart'. (7)

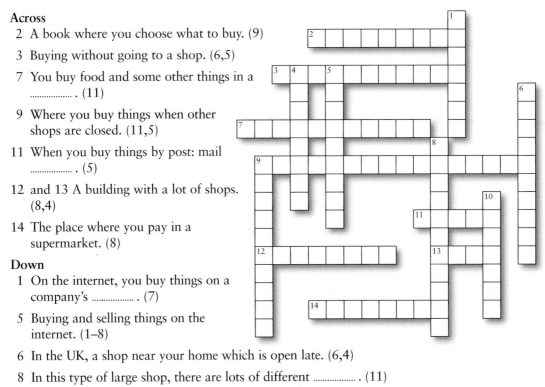

30.2 Complete the sentences. Look at A and B opposite to help you.

1 In a supermarket, you pay .... the checkout.

2 More and more books are sold .... the internet.

3 When you buy clothes .... mail order, you choose .... a catalogue.

4 You can order .... post or .... the phone.

Over to you

Do you like shopping? Where do you buy your clothes?

31 Where was it developed?

A The first PC

A journalist is interviewing Sandra Peters, an expert in the history of computers.

Journalist: Where **was** the first PC **developed**?
Sandra: It was **developed** at an IBM centre in Florida.

Journalist: Where was the software **written**?
Sandra: The software was written by Microsoft in California.

Journalist: Who was the PC **sold to**?
Sandra: It was sold to businesses and to people interested in computers.

It **was** They **were**	developed written	in	Florida. California.

To learn more about the past passive, see page 111.

B Where were the first PCs produced?

IBM PC (personal computer), 1981

Journalist: Where **were** the first PCs **produced**?
Sandra: PCs **were produced** at IBM's factories. But IBM allowed other companies to make the same computer with the same software.

Journalist: Which companies made PCs?
Sandra: At first, they were **made** by lots of companies, but today there are not so many: Dell, Gateway, Hewlett-Packard … . I still have a PC that was made by Compaq in 1987, but I don't use it now!

Journalist: Where was the first PC **manufactured**?
Sandra: The screen was made in Texas, the keyboard was manufactured in Mexico and the disks were produced in Singapore.

Journalist: And where was it all **put together**?
Sandra: In Texas. The PCs were **packed** there and then they were **distributed** all over the world.

31.1 Complete the table. Look at A and B opposite to help you. Use the verb list on page 00 if you need more help.

Base form (infinitive)	Third form (past participle)
develop	
distribute	
make	
manufacture	
pack	
put together	
sell	
write	

31.2 Complete the sentences using the correct form of the verb in brackets ( ). Look at A and B opposite to help you.

In the 1950s, Britain had a very big motorcycle industry. One of the companies was BSA.

1 The motorcycles were .... in the BSA factory. (put together)
2 Then they were .... by retailers all over the world. (sell)
3 They were .... by land and sea to different continents. (distribute)
4 They were .... into boxes. (pack)
5 BSA motorcycles were .... in Birmingham. (develop)

31.3 Now put the sentences (1–5) in 31.2 above into the correct order.

Over to you

Look at a product that you use every day. Where was it made? Where is it sold?

32 Product instructions

Follow the instructions

1 **Pull** the lever.

2 **Key in** your PIN number.

3 **Put** your ticket **into** the slot.

4 **Push** the door to open.

5 **Turn** the key to start.

6 **Plug** the cable **into** a socket.

7 **Insert** your card.

8 **Select** a language.

Press the button

To play a CD:

1 To **switch on**, press the 'On' button.

2 **Take** the CD **out of** the box.

3 **Put** the CD **into** the tray.

4 **Press** the 'Close' button.

5 Then press the 'Play' button.

6 To stop the disc, press the 'Stop' button.

32.1 Match the instructions in A opposite to the products and machines below.

a ticket barrier

b lemon squeezer

c cash machine
(3 instructions)

d car

e office door

f CD player

32.2 Now write the instructions for each of the products and machines in 32.1 above.

a ticket barrier   Put your ticket into the slot.
b lemon squeezer
c cash machine
d car
e office door
f CD player

32.3 Put the instructions for recording a DVD into the correct order. Look at B opposite to help you.

To record a DVD:

a When you have finished, press the 'Stop' button.

e Press the 'Record' button.

b Put a blank DVD into the tray.

f Press the 'On' button.

c Select the TV station that you want to record.

g Press the 'Open' button.

d Push the tray to close it.

Over to you
Give instructions for using an office drinks machine.

33 Problems with products

Faults

Antonia is having problems with her DVD player.
She phones the **call centre** (= office giving help on the
telephone) of the chain store where she bought it.

Sharon: **Service department**. How can I help?
Antonia: I **have a problem with** my DVD player.
           It **broke down** (= stopped working) last week.
Sharon: What **make and model number** is it?
Antonia: It's a Samson DVD 7000.
Sharon: What exactly is the **fault** (= technical problem)?
Antonia: When I press the button, the tray
           doesn't open.
Sharon: How old is the DVD player?
Antonia: I bought it last year.
Sharon: OK, you can **send it back** by post for **repair**
           (= the company will make it work again).
           Samson **guarantee** (= promise to repair or
           replace) their products for two years.
Antonia: That's difficult. I don't have the box.
Sharon: Don't worry. You can **take it back** to the shop.
           Where did you buy it? ...

> ### Samson DVD 7000
> Samson 2 year
> guarantee
>
> If you are not satisfied or have
> any problems with the DVD
> 7000, simply return to point
> of purchase along with this
> guarantee within 90 days and
> we will offer a replacement
> or full refund.

Guarantees

The company **repair** the DVD player and return it to Antonia, but it **breaks down** again.
She phones the call centre again.

Sharon: Service department. How can I help?
Antonia: My DVD player broke down last month. You repaired it, but it broke down
           again yesterday.
Sharon: What's the fault now?
Antonia: I can play DVDs, but I can't record.
Sharon: Is it still **under guarantee** (= in the time period of the guarantee)?
Antonia: Yes, I only bought it six months ago.
Sharon: OK. Because it's broken down again, we'll
           give you a **replacement** – a **brand new**
           (= completely new) machine.
Antonia: That's great!

33.1 Match the two parts of the sentences. Look at A and B opposite to help you.

1 This product is brand
2 This TV is still under
3 If you have a problem
4 My CD player broke
5 When my new phone stopped working, I sent it

a with your new kitchen equipment, just give us a call.
b down two days after I bought it!
c new. I bought it yesterday.
d back to the shop.
e guarantee. It's less than two years old.

33.2 Complete the sentences with words and phrases from the box. Look at A and B opposite to help you.

breaks down	call centre	guarantee	under guarantee
take it back	repair	replacement	fault

1 We .... our products for two years.

2 If the product doesn't work, ...
.... to the shop where you bought it.

3 If the shop can't help you, phone our ....
....

4 If there is still a ...., send the product back to
us. We will .... it.

5 If the product .... again while it is
still ...., send it back to us and we
will send you a ....

Over to you

Talk about a problem you had with a product. Did you:

■ send the product back for repair?   ■ get a new product?

What happened exactly?

34 Socializing 1: nice to meet you

A At the airport

Excuse me. Are you Rita Sandoro? I'm Stephanie Howard.

Hello. Nice to meet you.

Hello. Nice to meet you too.

How was the flight?

Very good thanks. No problems at all.

I'll take you to your hotel and then we'll go out to dinner.

Thank you. That would be nice

B At the office

Good morning, Rita. How are you?

Very well thanks, and you?

Fine thanks. Take a seat. Would you like something to drink? There's coffee, tea, and orange juice.

Juice, please.

Here you are.

Thank you.

Trevor, this is Rita Sandoro from World Wines in London. Rita, this is Trevor Smith, our marketing manager.

Nice to meet you, Rita.

Hello, Trevor. Pleased to meet you.

Have you been to Cape Town before?

No, this is my first visit.

Where are you staying?

At the Intercontinental.

What's it like?

Very comfortable, thanks.

C Saying goodbye

Stephanie:	It was nice meeting you, Rita.
Rita:	Nice meeting you too, Stephanie.
Stephanie:	Have a good trip back to London.
Rita:	Thanks. I'll be in touch soon.
Stephanie:	I look forward to seeing you next time.
Rita:	Yes, me too. Bye.
Stephanie:	Goodbye.

34.1 Choose the correct reply to each of the expressions (1–7). Look at A and B opposite to help you.

1 Nice to meet you.
  a Hello.
  b Fine, thanks.

2 How was the flight?
  a That would be nice.
  b Very good, thanks.

3 I'll take you to your hotel and then we can have dinner there.
  a Fine, thanks.
  b Thank you. That would be nice.

4 How are you?
  a Very well, thanks.
  b Nice to meet you.

5 It was nice meeting you.
  a Pleased to meet you.
  b Nice meeting you too.

6 I look forward to seeing you next time.
  a Yes, me too.
  b Here you are.

7 Have a good trip back.
  a Thanks.
  b That would be nice.

34.2 Complete the questions that two people ask a visitor. Look at B opposite to help you.

1 Leslie: Take a (1) .... Would you like (2) .... to drink? (3) .... coffee, tea, and apple juice.

2 Leslie: Brian, (4) .... is Georgina Osborne from SPL in Dublin. Georgina, this is Brian, our production manager.

3 Brian: Nice to meet you, Georgina. (5) .... you (6) .... to Melbourne before?

4 Brian: Where are you (7) .... ?

5 Brian: What's it (8) .... ?

34.3 Match Georgina's answers below to the questions (1–5) in 34.2 above. Look at B opposite to help you.

a At the Hilton.
b Pleased to meet you.
c Tea, please.
d Very comfortable, thanks.
e Yes, I was here about ten years ago.

Over to you

A visitor comes to your office. You introduce the visitor to a colleague. Write the conversation.

35 Socializing 2: at the restaurant

A Choosing and ordering

A table for two please.

Rita, do you smoke?

No, I don't.

What do you recommend?

Where would you like to sit – smoking or non-smoking?

Near the window in the non-smoking area, please.

The fish is very good. Do you like fish?

No, **I'm not keen on** (= I don't like) seafood. **What are you going to have?**

I think **I'll have** a chicken vindaloo. **That's** a type of curry **with** chicken.

Are you ready to order (= Are you ready to tell me what you want)?

That sounds good. I'll have the same.

Yes, I think so.

B Small talk

Do you live in London?

I commute too. It takes about 20 minutes by car. **Do you like** commuting?

It's fine, if there isn't too much traffic. **What do you do in your free time?**

Really? I play golf too! How about a game tomorrow after our meeting?

No, I live in Brighton, on the south coast. I commute. **What about you?**

It's OK if the train isn't late! I read, and I listen to music. **And you?**

I play a lot of golf.

Good idea!

C Thanking

Rita and Stephanie finish their meal.

Rita: **That was delicious!**

Stephanie: **I'm glad you liked it. Would you like** a coffee?

Rita: Yes please.

Stephanie (to waiter): Two coffees please.

(Later)

Stephanie: **Can we have the bill, please?**

Waiter: **Certainly.** *(The bill arrives)*

Stephanie (to Rita): **I'll get** (= pay for) **this**

Rita: **Thank you very much.**

Stephanie: **My pleasure!**

35.1 Put the conversation into the correct order. Look at A opposite to help you.

a Roxanne: What do you recommend? 1
b Francesca: I think I'll have a salade niçoise.
c Francesca: It's a type of salad with lots of different things in it.
d Francesca: The steak is very good. Do you like meat?
e Roxanne: I'm not keen on meat. What are you going to have?
f Roxanne: What's that?
g Roxanne: That sounds good. I'll have the same.

35.2 Match the questions (1–4) to the answers (a–d). Look at B opposite to help you.

1 Do you live in Paris?   **a** Good idea!

2 Do you like commuting?   **b** No, I live in Versailles, about 20 minutes from Paris.

3 What do you do in your free time?   **c** It's OK. I do a lot of work on the train.

4 How about a game this evening?   **d** I play squash.

35.3 Write the conversations below. Look at C opposite to help you.

1

Alain   Bengt

| Ask Bengt if he wants a dessert. |

| Say you would like ice cream. |

| Ask the waiter for two ice creams. |

| Say you liked the meal. |

| Reply. |

2

| Ask for the bill and tell Bengt that you will pay. |

| Thank Alain. |

| Reply. |

Over to you

You are at a restaurant with a visitor to your country. Write a 'small talk' conversation between yourself and the visitor.

A Starting informal calls

Hello.

Speaking.

Hello, Liam. How are you?

Is	Pia there?
	that Pia?

Hi Pia, it's Liam here.

B Starting formal calls

Good morning. Cara Thompson's office.

Hello.	Could Can	I speak to	Ms Thompson, **please?**

Who's calling, please?

My name's Julian Maxwell. **I'm calling from** JM Consultants in New York.

One moment please. I'll put you through.

Thank you.

Cara Thompson.

Good morning, Ms Thompson. My name's …

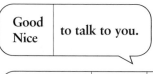

C Ending calls

I'll	phone call	again next week.

Good Nice	to talk to you.

See you	on Thursday. at the meeting. in Rome.

Thanks Thank you	for	calling. phoning.

Bye.
Goodbye.

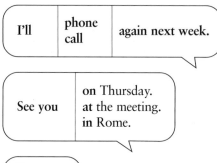

36.1 Put the conversation into the correct order. Look at A opposite to help you.

a Speaking!

b Is that Nadine?

c Hi Nadine, it's Mel here.

d Hi Mel. How are you?

e Hello.

36.2 Complete the conversation. Look at B opposite to help you.

Madeleine Townsend's PA   Fernando Soria   Madeleine Townsend

(1) .... Madeleine Townsend's office.

(2) .... Ms Townsend, (3) .... ?

Who's (4) .... , ... ?

(5) .... Fernando Soria.

I'll (6) ....

Thank you.

Madeleine Townsend.

36.3 Complete the conversation. Look at C opposite to help you.

So, you'll be in touch next week to fix the exact details?

Yes, I'll (1) ....

It was nice to talk to you.

Yes, (2) .... Thanks (3) ....

(4) .... in Paris. Goodbye.

(5) ....

Over to you

When you answer the phone at work, what do you say?
Write short dialogues for the beginning of a phone conversation at work:
■ with someone you know.
■ with someone you don't know.

37 Telephoning 2: spelling and numbers

A Telephone alphabet

When someone **spells** (= says how to write) a word on the phone, it can be difficult to hear the difference between these letters:

- B and P
- B and V
- D and T
- F and S
- I and Y
- M and N

Make sure you learn the English names for these letters:

- A and R
- E and I
- O and U
- I and Y
- C and S
- G and J
- K and Q
- V and W

To learn more about how to pronounce each letter, see page 106.

If you want to spell a word you can say **A for Alpha**, using the **telephone alphabet** in this list.

Alpha	Bravo	Charlie	Delta	Echo	Foxtrot
Golf	Hotel	India	Juliet	Kilo	Lima
Mike	November	Oscar	Papa	Quebec	Romeo
Sierra	Tango	Uniform	Victor	Whisky	X-ray
Yankee	Zulu				

B Spelling

Who's calling please?

My name's Nora Laker.

Can you spell that, please?

Yes, it's Nora: N for November, O for Oscar, R for Romeo, A for Alpha. I'm calling from Maggs Lind, in London.

Is that M-A-G-S?

No, M-A-**double G-S**, **new word**, Lind – L-I-N-D.

C Numbers

You say telephone numbers in groups of numbers. Your voice goes up for each group, except for the last group, when your voice goes down.

00	44	20	9422	5483
Double oh	double four	two oh	nine four double two	five four eight three

00	1	212	131	6544
Zero zero	one	two one two	one three one	six five four four

> BrE: double oh;
> AmE: zero zero

37.1 You are talking about numbers and letters on the telephone. Use the telephone alphabet to correct the other person. Look at A opposite to help you.

WR51 LMB

32D876

NEW YORK
CLP 933

W.R.CYCLES
REF: 9855 N

934 HUY 75

Model 433F

1 Is that V for Victor?
   No, B for Bravo.

2 Is that T for Tango?

3 Is that B for Bravo?

4 Is that M for Mike?

5 Is that I for India?

6 Is that S for Sierra?

37.2 Look at the telephone list for a company's staff around the world. Spell the names using the telephone alphabet, then use arrows above the numbers to show how your voice goes up and down. Look at A opposite to help you.

1 Mr Caire   00 33 1 9422 5122
   C for Charlie, A for Alpha, I for India, R for Romeo, E for Echo

2 Professor Fanshaw   00 44 131 937 9821

3 Ms Petersson   00 46 8 487 5044

4 Mr Hanks   00 1 918 324 6622

5 Doctor Tanawa   00 81 42 975 2349

6 Ms Dos Santos   00 55 61 648 7785

37.3 Match the questions to the answers. Look at B opposite to help you.

1 Who's calling, please?

2 Can you spell that, please?

3 Which company are you phoning from?

4 Is that C-O-L-I-N-S?

a No, C-O-double L-I-N-S.

b John Collins and Associates.

c T for Tango, A for Alpha, N for November, Y for Yankee, A for Alpha, new word, H for Hotel, U for Umbrella, double L for Lima.

d Tanya Hull.

Over to you

Spell your name, your home address and your company address. Use the telephone alphabet. What are your phone numbers at home, at work and on your mobile? Say them with the correct intonation.

A Showing understanding

Showing you understand

I'm phoning from UWX in Sydney.

Right.

Could you ask Ellen to email the details?

OK. I'll do that.

It's very important.

I understand.

B Checking and confirming information

Checking

My name's Nicholls.

Sorry, I didn't get that. Could you speak more slowly, please?

I'm sorry. My – name – is – Nicholls.

Is that one L or two?

Two. N-I-C-H-O-double L-S.
The company is Goodwood.

Can you spell that please?

I'm calling from Bendrix in London.

Can you repeat that (= say it again), **please?**

Yes, it's Bendrix.

Sorry, I can't hear you. Could you speak up (= speak more loudly), **please?**

Yes, of course. The number is 020 7400 3004.

So, that's 020 7400 3004.

Confirming

| That's | it. |
| | right. |

Jane Nicholls
jane.nicholls@jhu.co.uk

My email address is
Jane **dot** Nicholls **at** jhu **dot** co **dot** uk.
/kəʊ/

38.1 What do you say in the situations below? Look at A and B opposite to help you.

    1 You understand what the caller is saying. (3 expressions)
    2 The other person is speaking too fast.
    3 You can't hear the other person.
    4 You're not sure how to write a name.
    5 You want someone to say the word again.
    6 You confirm some information.

38.2 Put the conversation into the correct order. Look at B opposite to help you. The first sentence is i.

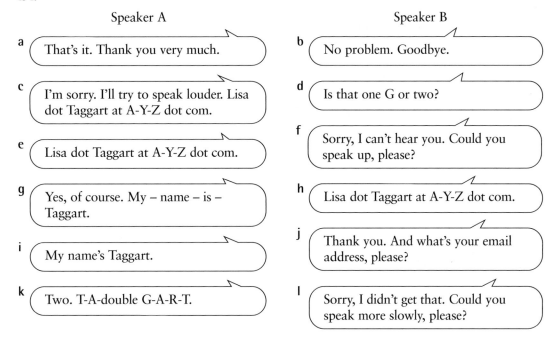

Speaker A

a That's it. Thank you very much.

c I'm sorry. I'll try to speak louder. Lisa dot Taggart at A-Y-Z dot com.

e Lisa dot Taggart at A-Y-Z dot com.

g Yes, of course. My – name – is – Taggart.

i My name's Taggart.

k Two. T-A-double G-A-R-T.

Speaker B

b No problem. Goodbye.

d Is that one G or two?

f Sorry, I can't hear you. Could you speak up, please?

h Lisa dot Taggart at A-Y-Z dot com.

j Thank you. And what's your email address, please?

l Sorry, I didn't get that. Could you speak more slowly, please?

38.3 Write the conversation below. Look at B opposite to help you.

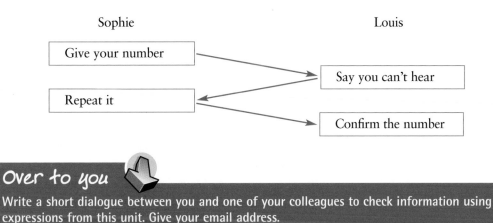

Sophie

Give your number

Repeat it

Louis

Say you can't hear

Confirm the number

Over to you

Write a short dialogue between you and one of your colleagues to check information using expressions from this unit. Give your email address.

A Useful expressions

Person receiving a call

| I'm sorry,
I'm afraid | he's
she's | on another call.
not here at the moment. |

| Can I take a message? (= you want to write down a message from the caller) |
| Who's calling please? |
| Which company are you calling from? |

Person making a call

| Can
Could | I leave a message? (= you want to give a message) |

| Can
Could | you ask | him
her | to | call
phone | me back | tomorrow?
as soon as possible? |

B Leaving a message

Person receiving a call   **Person making a call**

Mark Simpson's office.

> Hello. Can I speak to Mr Simpson please?

I'm sorry, he's in a meeting. Can I take a message?

> Yes, please. My name's Denise Parker.

Can I have your number?

> Yes, it's 020 9422 5483.

020 9422 …

> 5483.

5483. So, that's 020 9422 5483.

> That's right. Could you ask him to call me back? It's very urgent (= important to do quickly).

I'll give him the message.

> Thank you very much. Goodbye.

Goodbye.

39.1 Put this conversation into the correct order. Look at A and B opposite to help you. The first sentence is h.

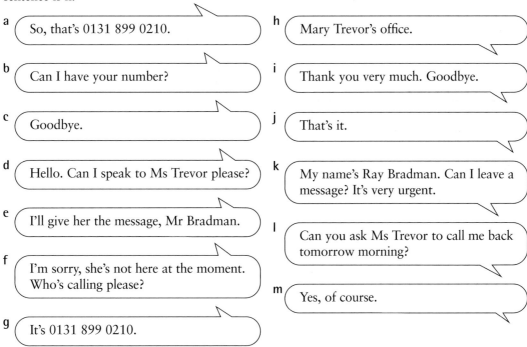

a So, that's 0131 899 0210.

b Can I have your number?

c Goodbye.

d Hello. Can I speak to Ms Trevor please?

e I'll give her the message, Mr Bradman.

f I'm sorry, she's not here at the moment. Who's calling please?

g It's 0131 899 0210.

h Mary Trevor's office.

i Thank you very much. Goodbye.

j That's it.

k My name's Ray Bradman. Can I leave a message? It's very urgent.

l Can you ask Ms Trevor to call me back tomorrow morning?

m Yes, of course.

39.2 Complete the message form using the information from the call in 39.1 above.

TELEPHONE MESSAGE

Message for: _____

Name of caller: _____

☐ **Will call again** ☐ **Please call**

Phone number: _____

☐ **Urgent** ☐ **Not urgent**

Notes: _____

_____

Over to you

Think of the last phone message that you left. What did you say? Practise saying it in English.

40 Email, faxes and letters 1: business writing

A Ways of communicating

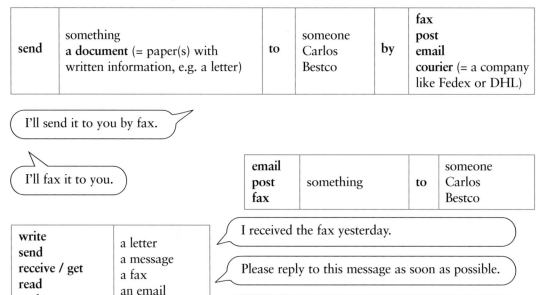

send	something **a document** (= paper(s) with written information, e.g. a letter)	to	someone Carlos Bestco	by	**fax** **post** **email** **courier** (= a company like Fedex or DHL)

> I'll send it to you by fax.

> I'll fax it to you.

email **post** **fax**	something	to	someone Carlos Bestco

write **send** **receive / get** **read** **reply to**	a letter a message a fax an email

> I received the fax yesterday.

> Please reply to this message as soon as possible.

> I get over 50 emails every day.

B Formal and informal

If you know someone well, you use an **informal** style. If you don't know the person or the communication is very serious or official, you use a **formal** style. You need to think about **formality** when you begin and end your writing.

C Beginnings

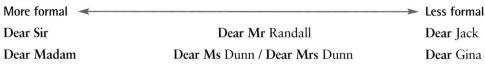

More formal ←——————————————————→ Less formal

Dear Sir	**Dear Mr** Randall	**Dear** Jack
Dear Madam	**Dear Ms** Dunn / **Dear Mrs** Dunn	**Dear** Gina

Note: You use 'Dear Sir' for a man, and 'Dear Madam' for a woman, when you don't know the person's name.

D Endings

More formal ←——————————————————→ Less formal

Best regards	**Regards**	**Best wishes**	**All the best**	**Best**
Yours sincerely				
Yours faithfully			**Yours**	

Note: You use 'Yours faithfully' only in BrE, when you don't know the person's name.

BrE: Yours sincerely;
AmE: Sincerely

40.1 Choose the correct word to complete each sentence. Look at A opposite to help you.

1 I've .... (written/got) five faxes this morning, but I haven't sent them yet.
2 I .... (replied/received) her letter yesterday.
3 There's no need to .... (read/reply) to this email.
4 I .... (got/posted) this email from Rita.
5 I've .... (written/read) your message, but I haven't .... (replied/sent) to it yet.
6 I'll .... (fax/reply) the information to her.

40.2 Kay Lumsden receives the messages below (1–5). Are they formal (F) or informal (I)? Look at B opposite to help you.

1 Her colleague, Tom, asks Kay if she's free for lunch.   I
2 A journalist (Tony Kent) writes to ask her for an interview.
3 Her friend, Serena, asks Kay if she's free for a game of tennis.
4 A supplier that she doesn't know (Roger Olafsson) writes to ask Kay for a meeting.
5 Janet Freeman, who doesn't know Kay's name, writes to ask for a job.

40.3 Write the beginning and ending of each message (1–5) in 40.2 above. Look at B, C and D opposite to help you.

1 (beginning) Dear Kay ....
  (ending) .... Best wishes ....
  .... Tom ....

2 (beginning) ....
  (ending) ....
  ....

3 (beginning) ....
  (ending) ....
  ....

4 (beginning) ....
  (ending) ....
  ....

5 (beginning) ....
  (ending) ....
  ....

Over to you

How do you prefer to communicate:

■ with friends?   ■ with colleagues?   ■ with clients?

41 Email, faxes and letters 2: the message

Starting the message

Thanking someone

| Thank you (very much) (Many) thanks | for | your email. a very useful meeting yesterday. |
| | | **coming** to Prague yesterday. **sending** the information I asked for. |

Giving a reason for writing

| I'm writing This (email/fax/letter) is | to | **let you know** our new contact details. **tell you that** I'm coming to Boston next month. **confirm** (= make sure you know) the details of my trip. |

Future action

Would it be possible to postpone the meeting?

Could you send us the information as soon as possible?

Can you call me next week?

| I look forward | to | **hearing from you** (= receiving your reply). **seeing** you in Budapest. **meeting** your colleagues next week. |

I'll speak to you next week.

I'll call you as soon as possible.

Please let me know if you need anything else.

Enclosures and attachments

Something that you send with a letter is an **enclosure**. Something that you send with an email or a fax is an **attachment**. You can write:

| Please find enclosed I'm enclosing Please find attached I'm attaching | a | **brochure** (= pictures and information about a company or product). **map** (= a drawing to show where places are). **photo.** **report** (= a document describing a particular subject). |

41.1 Complete the message. Look at A and B opposite to help you.

> Dear Ms Howard
>
> (1) .... agreeing to see me next week. (2) ....
> .... confirm details of my trip: I'm flying from London on
> Thursday afternoon, 26 July, and staying at the Hilton in the centre of Cape Town.
> (3) .... send me a map showing where your company is?
>
> (4) .... attaching some information about my company, World Wine Imports.
> Please (5) .... if you need any more information about
> the company before the meeting.
>
> I (6) .... to hearing from you.
>
> Yours sincerely
>
> Rita Sandoro

41.2 Match the situations (1–6) to the sentences (a–f). Look at C opposite to help you.

1 You send a photo with an email.

2 You send information about your products with a letter.

3 You send a drawing to show your company's location with an email.

4 You send a document about a particular subject with a fax.

5 You send a drawing to show your company's location with a letter.

6 You send information about a particular subject with a letter.

a I'm enclosing some brochures.

b Please find attached a map.

c I'm attaching a report.

d I'm attaching a picture of our product.

e Please find enclosed a report.

f I'm enclosing a map.

Over to you

Write a message to an important client who is visiting your company next week, and send a map to show where your company is. Remember to use formal language.

A Email language

forward		= send an email that you have received to someone else
delete	an email	= remove an email from your computer
copy		= send a copy of an email to other people at the same time

> Could you forward Rita's email to me?

> Don't delete the email – it's important

> I'm sending the information to John by email – I'll copy it to you.

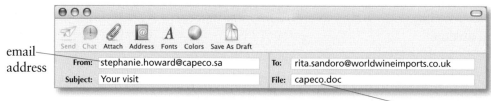

email address

From: stephanie.howard@capeco.sa   To: rita.sandoro@worldwineimports.co.uk
Subject: Your visit   File: capeco.doc

attachment

To learn more about how to say email addresses, see Unit 38.
To learn more about attachments, see Unit 41.

B Informal emails

Sometimes emails are written quickly and are very informal. Here are some of the things you see in informal emails:

Informal

> **Hi** Rita
> **Pleased to hear** that you're coming to Cape Town next Tuesday. **I'll** come and pick you up at the airport.
> **Here's** the brochure we talked about.
> **See you v. soon!**
> **Best**
> Stephanie

Formal

> **Dear** Ms Sandoro
> **I am pleased to hear** that you are coming to Cape Town on 25 July. **I will** come and pick you up at the airport.
> **Please find attached** the brochure you requested.
> **I look forward to meeting you.**
> **Yours sincerely**
> Stephanie Howard

- ■ **abbreviations**   v. = very
- ■ **contractions**   I'll = I will
- ■ **missing words**   Pleased to hear = I am pleased to hear

C Beginnings and endings

If you know someone very well, you can start and end the email with very informal language. Sometimes you start the message with **Hi** or **Hello**, or the person's name.

> **Hi** Rita
> Here are the documents you requested.
> **Best**
> Stephanie

> **Stephanie**
> Thanks for the documents!
> **Rita**

To learn more about formal and informal beginnings and endings, see Unit 40.

42.1 Complete the email with words from the box. Look at A opposite to help you.

Attachment	deleted	email address	Cc (= copy)
forward	To	Subject	From

```
● ● ●                                                                ⬭
 ✈  ☺  📎  @  A  ⬤  📄
Send Chat Attach Address Fonts Colors Save As Draft

...................: markwalker@bestco.uk        ...................: tomhill@bestco.uk

...................: davidjames@bestco.uk         ...................: Request for information

...................: Sales report.doc

Dear Tom
I'm attaching the report you requested. Could you ..................... it to Sarah? I don't
know her ..................... ..................... – I think I ..................... it by mistake! I'm copying this
email to David too.
Best wishes
Mark
```

42.2 Change the sentences from formal to informal. Look at B opposite to help you.

1 I enjoyed meeting you last week. (missing word)
   <u>Enjoyed meeting you last week.</u>

2 I am so glad you had a nice trip back to London. (contraction)
   ....

3 I have posted the brochure to you. (contraction)
   ....

4 They are very interested in working with you. (abbreviation)
   ....

42.3 Change the sentences from informal to formal. Look at B opposite to help you.

1 We're arriving in London on Monday. (contraction)
   ....

2 It was v. good to speak to you yesterday. (abbreviation)
   ....

3 Hope that your hotel is comfortable. (missing word)
   ....

4 I'll be in touch again soon. (contraction)
   ....

Over to you

Write the text of an email with an attachment:

◾ to send to a colleague.   ◾ to send to a customer.

Think about formal and informal language.

43 Presentations 1: getting started

A Preparation

Jennifer Marshall is an expert in **presentation skills**. She gives this advice:

Start to **prepare** (= get ready) early.

Think about your **audience** (= the people who will be at your presentation).

Write **notes**.

Prepare **slides**.

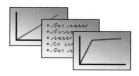

Prepare **handouts** (= pages with information for the audience).

Check the room (= make sure the room is ready).

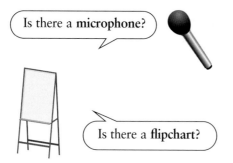

Is there a **microphone**?

Is there a **projector**?

Is there a **flipchart**?

Is there a **whiteboard**?

B Introduction

Introducing yourself and your subject

> **My name's** ....
> **I work for** Gillette. **I work in the** sales **department**.
> **Today I'm going to talk about** ...

Describing the plan

First Then After that Next Finally	I'll I'd like to	look at say something about move on to	sales. our products.

Talking about questions

If you have any questions,	**please feel free to interrupt me** (= stop me while I'm talking). **I'll be happy to answer them at the end.**

Business Vocabulary in Use (elementary)

43.1 Complete the sentences from a presentation. Look at B opposite to help you.

1 Finally, I'll say something .... the future – I'll talk about possible new products for the next ten years.
2 First, I'll look .... business-to-business products.
3 Hello. My name's Ron Grant. I work .... GIE, the electronics company.
4 Then, I'll move .... consumer products.
5 Today I'm going to talk .... our latest business-to-business and consumer products.

43.2 Lisa Woo, the marketing manager at Samson, is going to give a presentation. Write what she needs. Look at A opposite to help you.

1 I want to be sure everyone can hear me.
I need a ..microphone.. .

2 I want to write on paper so that everyone can see.
I need a ....

3 I want to know if there are enough chairs.
I need to ....

4 I want to use my computer to show information.
I need a ....

5 The audience doesn't want extra information on paper.
I don't need ....

43.3 Put the sentences of Lisa's introduction into the correct order. Look at B opposite to help you.

a And finally, I'll say something about how we can work with your company.
b First, I'll look at the technical side.
c I work for Samson in the marketing department.
d If you have any questions, I'll be happy to answer them at the end of my presentation.
e My name's Lisa Woo.
f Then, I'll move on to the sales possibilities.
g Today I'm going to talk about a new product that we have developed.

Over to you

Write the introduction to a presentation and practise reading it aloud.

A Sections

Presentations are usually divided into **sections** (= parts).

To start a section or move on to a new section

First Firstly		look at look at move on to turn to	the products. the sales figures.		
Second Secondly Third Now	let's I'd like to		the	next	point. area.
Finally				last	

B Slides and handouts

To talk about a slide or a handout

As you can see in Let's look at	**this slide** of last year's sales … **the handout** about our products …

C Ending and questions

To end the presentation

> That is the end of my presentation.

> Thank you very much.

> Thank you for listening.

> Thank you for coming.

Questions

> Are there any questions?

> If you have any questions, I'll be happy to answer them now.

> I'm sorry, but I didn't follow your question.

> Could you repeat the question?

> I'm sorry, but I don't know the answer to that. Can I check and get back to you?

> I'm sorry, but I can't give you that information.

44.1 Samson's marketing manager is making a presentation. Look at her plan and write what she says at the start of each section. Look at A and C opposite to help you.

Plan

1 Technical side

2 Sales plan (show slide)

3 Samson's branches

4 Ending

5 Questions

1 First, I'd like to talk about the technical side.
2 ....
3 ....
4 ....
5 ....

44.2 What do you say in the situations below? Look at C opposite to help you.

1 You don't understand a question.
I'm sorry, but I didn't follow your question.
2 You can't answer a question because the information is confidential.
....
3 You are ready to answer questions.
....
4 You want someone to say the question again.
....
5 You don't know the answer.
....
6 You want to find some information and answer a question later.
....

Over to you

Write one of the sections of the presentation that you started in 'Over to you' in the previous unit.

Pie charts

This **pie chart** shows where people from Estland had their summer holiday last year.

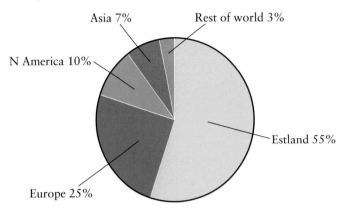

This segment **The** red **segment** **The segment shaded** blue	shows	that … the number of … the percentage of …

This segment shows that most people stayed in Estland for their summer holiday.

The blue segment shows the number of people who went to Europe – 25 per cent.

Graphs and bar charts

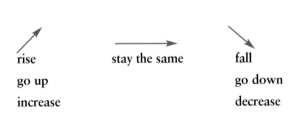

rise
go up
increase

stay the same

fall
go down
decrease

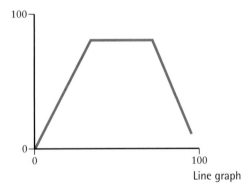

Line graph

This **bar graph** or **bar chart** shows sales of Samson phones from January to June last year.

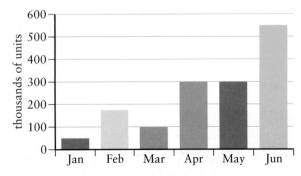

In January last year, Samson sold 50,000 phones. In February, sales **rose to** 175,000. Sales in March **fell from** 175,000 **to 100,000 units**. In April, sales **increased by** 200,000 units to 300,000 units and in May they **stayed the same**. Then in June, sales **went up by** 250,000 units to 550,000 units.

45.1 Complete and label the pie chart showing the information below. Look at A opposite to help you.

Cars sold in Estland last year

Model	Number sold	Percentage of total
Delta	4.5 million	45%
Echo	2.5 million	25%
Alpha	2 million	20%
Others	1 million	10%
Total	10 million cars	100%

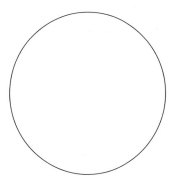

Now write a sentence about one of the segments.

....

45.2 Complete the table. Look at C opposite to help you. Use the verb list on page 112 if you need more help.

Base form (infinitive)	Second form (past simple)
	decreased
	went down
	fell
	increased
	rose
	stayed the same

45.3 Complete the text describing the bar graph. Look at B opposite to help you.

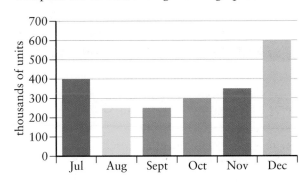

Sales of Samson mobile phones from July to December last year

In July last year, Samson sold 400,000 phones. In August, sales (1) .... to 250,000. Sales in September (2) .... In October, sales increased (3) .... 50,000 units to 300,000 units and in November they rose (4) .... 300,000 (5) .... 350,000 units. Then in December, sales went (6) .... by 250,000 units to 600,000 units.

Over to you

Draw a bar graph showing how many days off you have each month in a typical year, and describe it. (Include holidays and days off for illness.)

46 Presentations 4: site tours

A Company sites

At Samson's **main** (= most important) **site** you can find:

the reception area	where visitors arrive
the offices	where people work on managing and planning
the factory or **manufacturing plant**	where products are made
the research and development department	where people work on new ideas and products
the training department	where employees learn how to do their work

B Introduction to the tour

Guide: Good morning, ladies and gentlemen, and **welcome to** Samson. Today, **we're going to see** some of the departments on this site. **We'll start** here in the reception area, **then I'll show you** the main departments and **finally we'll look at** the production area. **I'm afraid we don't allow photography during the tour.**

C Guided tour

Guide: **Let's now leave** the reception area and **move on to** the offices. **Come this way, please.**

Here **on the left you can see** the marketing department and **on the right,** the finance department. **This is** the finance director, Clara Long.

Clara Long: Hello, everyone.

Guide: **Follow me** and **let's go** into the manufacturing plant. **This is where** we make our mobile phones. We make a million phones a year in this plant.

Let's continue now to the research and development department. **I'm afraid this area is** restricted (= closed to the public) but **as you can see** through the window, we're testing new designs for our phones.

Now, finally, we can go to **have a look at** the training department. This is where we do all the company training. **In this room,** you can see some of our managers from the finance department on a course in advanced finance. **Can I ask you to keep your voices down** (= speak more quietly) **in this area?**

46.1 Match each place (1–5) to what the guide says (a–e) during the guided tour of a company. Look at A opposite to help you.

1 The factory   a We work on ideas for our new products here.

2 The offices   b This is where people learn how to do their job.

3 The training department   c This is where we make the products.

4 The reception area   d This is where our managers work.

5 The research and development   e We welcome company visitors here.
   department

46.2 You are the guide on a company site tour. What do you say in the situations below? Look at B and C opposite to help you.

1 Ask your visitors to speak more quietly.
2 Tell them to follow you into the finance department.
3 Say that they cannot take photos.
4 Tell them that the company's machines are on the left.
5 Explain that they cannot go into room 101.

46.3 Complete the site tour using the map below. Look at B and C opposite to help you.

We'll start here in the reception area. Can I ask you to keep your voices (1) ......*down*...... in this area? Let's now leave the reception area and (2) .... on to the offices. Come this (3) .... , please. Here on the (4) .... you can see the sales department and on the (5) .... , the human resources department.

Let's (6) .... now to the research and development department. This is where we design new computers. Finally, we can go to have a (7) .... at the training department. This is where we do all the company training, including English classes for our employees.

I'm sorry, but we can't go into the manufacturing plant. It's (8) .... and closed to the public. Are there any questions?

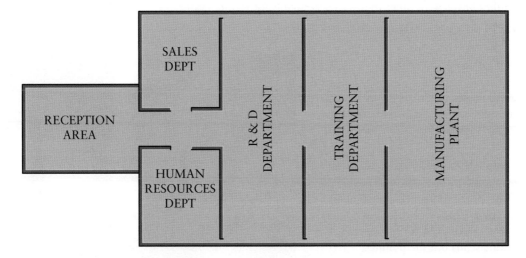

Over to you

Write the beginning of a guided tour for your site. Welcome the people to the company and name the places you are going to visit. Then write what you say when you take them to the first place.

47 Meetings 1: organizing a meeting

A Word combinations with 'meeting'

These verbs are often used in front of 'a meeting'.

arrange		= organize a meeting
chair		= be in charge of a meeting
attend	a meeting	= go to a meeting
miss		= not go to a meeting
postpone		= change a meeting to a later time
cancel		= not have a planned meeting

B Agendas

An **agenda** is a list of **items** (= different things) to talk about at a meeting. Before the meeting, someone **sends out the agenda** (= sends copies to everyone attending).

> ### AGENDA
> Staff meeting, 25 January 20_ _ , Meeting room 3
>
> Apologies for absence
> **Minutes** of the last meeting
> 1 Car parking
> 2 Company restaurant
> 3 Holiday dates
> 4 **AOB**

any other business (= other things that people want to talk about)
venue (= the place where the meeting will be)

C Apologies and minutes

If you cannot attend a meeting, you **send your apologies** (= a message to say you cannot attend). At the beginning of the meeting, someone reads out these messages.

The **minutes** of a meeting are written notes of what is said and decided in the meeting. During the meeting, someone **takes the minutes** (= writes down what is said and decided). After the meeting, someone **sends out the minutes**.

At the beginning of the next meeting people agree that the minutes are correct.

47.1 Choose the correct word to complete each sentence. Look at A opposite to help you.

1 She .... (missed/arranged) the meeting because she was late for work.
2 I decided to .... (cancel/arrange) the meeting because there was nothing to discuss.
3 We can .... (postpone/cancel) the meeting until next week if necessary.
4 I asked Jean to .... (arrange/miss) the meeting next week but there were no rooms available.
5 They .... (attended/postponed) the meeting, but they didn't hear anything interesting.
6 This meeting is very important. Don't .... (miss/attend) it!

47.2 Make phrases using the verbs and nouns below. Then match the phrases to their meanings (1–4). Look at A and B opposite to help you.

attend	your apologies
send	the minutes
send out	the agenda
take	a meeting

1 make the formal record of a meeting
2 give people a list of things to talk about at a meeting
3 go to a meeting
4 say that you will not be able to come to a meeting

47.3 Complete the memo with words from the box. Look at B opposite to help you.

venue	minutes	items	attend	agenda

MEMO

From: Chief Executive
To: All managers

Please find enclosed the (1) .... for next week's meeting.
Please make a note of the (2) ....: we are meeting in room 7.
Let me know if you are unable to (3) ....
Please bring with you a copy of the (4) .... of the last meeting.
If you want me to add other (5) .... to the agenda, please let me know.

Over to you

Write the agenda for a meeting in your organization, showing the date, the venue, and the items to talk about.

48 Meetings 2: chairing a meeting

A Chairing

The **chairman, chairwoman** or **chair** (= the person in charge of the meeting) **opens, runs** (= manages) and **closes** the meeting.

Opening the meeting

> Is everybody ready? Let's make a start.

> Does everyone agree with the minutes of the last meeting?

> James and Chris **send their apologies.**

Running the meeting

> So, **the first item** is the company car park.

> **Let's move on to** the next item: the company restaurant.

Closing the meeting

> **Can I sum up** (= repeat the main ideas)? We decided …

> I think that's all for today. Thank you for coming. See you at the next meeting.

B Interrupting and stopping interruptions

Interrupting

Can	I Isabella	say something come in	here?

Stopping interruptions

Just a moment.	I haven't finished … Can I just finish? Let him / her finish.

> Can I say something here about the costs?

> Just a moment. I haven't finished talking about the plans.

48.1 Complete the sentences. Look at A and B opposite to help you.

1 That's all .... today.
2 Thank you .... coming.
3 Let's talk about it .... the next meeting.
4 Let's move .... to the next item.
5 Can I sum .... ?
6 Does everyone agree .... the minutes .... the last meeting?
7 Can I come .... here?

48.2 You are chairing a meeting. What do you say in the situations below?

1 You want Val to let Yvonne speak.

....

2 You want Val to let Yvonne finish.

....

3 You start the meeting.

....

4 You say that Tanya and Stefan are sorry that they cannot attend.

....

5 You repeat the most important ideas.

....

6 You ask if everyone agrees with the minutes.

....

7 You end the meeting and thank people for coming.

....

8 You introduce the first item – the company's new restaurant.

....

 Over to you

Think about a recent meeting you attended. Write down what the chair said to open, run and close the meeting. Use some of the expressions in this unit and in Unit 47.

49 Meetings 3: opinions and explanations

A Opinions, agreeing and disagreeing

An **opinion** is what a person thinks about an idea or a subject. If you have the same opinion as another person, then you **agree**. If you have a different opinion, you **disagree**.

Asking for opinions

What do you think	about …?
What's your opinion	of …?

Giving opinions

I think …
In my opinion, …

Agreeing

I agree.	
Exactly.	
That's right.	
I agree with Peter on	that.
	this.

Disagreeing

I don't agree.	
I'm afraid I disagree.	
Yes, but …	
I disagree with Sue on	that.
	this.

A: *What's your opinion of the service in the company restaurant?*
B: *I think it's very bad!*
C: *I agree. It's so slow.*
D: *I'm afraid I disagree. In my opinion, it's quite good.*

B Suggesting and explaining

Suggesting (= telling people about an idea or a plan)

(How about …?)   (What about …?)

(Why don't we …?)   (I have an idea. Let's …)

Responding

(That's a good idea.)

Asking for explanation

(Sorry, I don't understand. Do you mean that …?)   (Are you saying that …?)

A: *I disagree with D on this. We need to find new people to work in the restaurant.*
B: *Can I come in here? I have an idea. Let's use a company from outside.*
C: *Sorry, I don't understand. Do you mean that the people working in the restaurant will not be employees of our company?*
B: *That's right. The restaurant company can be completely independent.*
A: *That's a good idea!*
D: *I don't agree. We'll lose control of the restaurant!*

49.1 Complete the conversation from a meeting using the phrases (a–g). Look at A and B opposite to help you.

a I have an idea
b I disagree with Ben
c That's a good idea
d Yes, but
e Do you mean
f That's right
g what do you think

Anna: So, who's the best person for the job? Ben, (1) .... ?
Ben: Lea Smith is very good. She has a lot of experience.
Charlene: (2) .... about this. Malcolm Jones may be younger, but he has a lot of experience too.
Ben: (3) .... Lea can start work next week. Malcolm can only start next month.
Dan: Can I come in here? (4) .... We can give them both a job as a sort of test for six months.
Ella: (5) .... keep them both for six months and then give one of them the permanent job?
Dan: (6) ....
Anna: (7) .... ! I hadn't thought of that.

49.2 Match what happens in the meeting (1–7) to what the people say (a–g). Look at A and B opposite to help you.

1 Naomi interrupts, and agrees with Linda.

2 Manuel gives his opinion.

3 Manuel makes a suggestion.

4 Linda disagrees with Manuel.

5 The chair, Chris, starts the meeting.

6 The chair asks for Manuel's opinion.

7 Chris responds.

a I have an idea. Let's tell them we will order more products if they can make the delivery more reliable.

b I think Partco's products are very cheap.

c What do you think about Partco, Manuel?

d Is everybody ready?

e Yes, but they never deliver on time.

f That's a good idea.

g Can I say something here? I agree with Linda – deliveries from Partco are always late.

49.3 Now put the sentences (a–g) in 49.2 above into the correct order.

Over to you

Think again about a recent meeting you attended. Write what people said to agree and disagree. Use some of the expressions in this unit.

Pronunciation of the alphabet

a   /eɪ/

b   /biː/

c   /siː/

d   /diː/

e   /iː/

f   /ef/

g   /dʒiː/

h   /eɪtʃ/

i   /aɪ/

j   /dʒeɪ/

k   /keɪ/

l   /el/

m   /em/

n   /en/

o   /əʊ/

p   /piː/

q   /kjuː/

r   /aː/

s   /es/

t   /tiː/

u   /juː/

v   /viː/

w   /ˈdʌbljuː/

x   /eks/

y   /waɪ/

z   /zed/

Verbs 1: present simple

Form

- You make the present simple with the base form (= infinitive).
- You add -*s* to the base form for 'he', 'she' and 'it' (= third person).
- With some verbs, for example 'go' and 'do', you add -*es* to the base form.

Affirmative sentences

I You	work.
He She It	works.
We They	work.

Negative sentences

I You	do not don't	
He She It	does not doesn't	work.
We They	do not don't	

Question forms

Do	I you	
Does	he she it	work?
Do	we they	

Where When Why How	do	I you	
	does	he she it	work?
	do	we they	

Examples

Which department does she work in? (Unit 7)

Some people work 20 hours a week. (Unit 8)

Do you commute? (Unit 10)

He explains things very clearly. (Unit 13)

She doesn't have computer skills. (Unit 13)

I play the piano, but not very often. (Unit 20)

How do you try to save money? (Unit 24)

When I press the button, the tray doesn't open. (Unit 33)

Verbs 2: present continuous

Form

■ You make the present continuous with 'be' + the -ing form of the verb.

Affirmative sentences

I am I'm	
You are You're	
He is He's	
She is She's	working.
It It's	
We are We're	
They are They're	

Negative sentences

I am not I'm not	
You are not You aren't	
He is not He isn't	
She is not She isn't	working.
It is not It isn't	
We are not We aren't	
They are not They aren't	

Question forms

Am I Are you	
Is he Is she Is it	working?
Are we	
Are they	

Where When Why How	am I are you is he is she is it are we are they	working?

Examples

How are things going? (Unit 12)

What are you doing on Friday? (Unit 19)

I'm going to a sales meeting on Friday. (Unit 19)

Are you renting or buying your house? (Unit 24)

Verbs 3: past simple

Form

- You make the past simple of regular verbs with the base form (= infinitive) + -ed or -d.

- For most regular verbs you add -ed. For verbs ending in -e, you add -d.

- Some verbs are irregular (= do not follow this pattern). For irregular past simple forms, see page 112.

Affirmative sentences

I You He She It We They	worked.

Negative sentences

I You He She It We They	did not didn't	work.

Question forms

Did	I you he she it we they	work?

Where When Why How	did	I you he she it you the	work?

Examples

His mother worked at a furniture company. (Unit 12)

What did his parents do? (Unit 12)

When did he leave school? (Unit 12)

I bought it last year. (Unit 33)

Did you send the product back for repair? (Unit 33)

I didn't get that. (Unit 38)

In June, sales went up by 250,000 units. (Unit 45)

Verbs 4: present passive

Form

- You make the present passive with 'is' or 'are' + the past participle (= third form) of the verb.
- Some verbs are irregular. For irregular past participle forms, see page 112.

They sell the products in supermarkets.

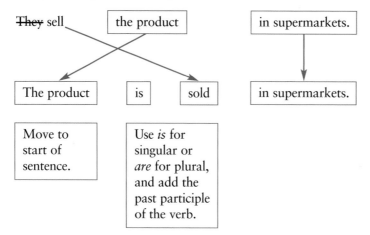

Affirmative sentences

The product / It	is	sold in supermarkets.
The products / They	are	sold in supermarkets.

Negative sentences

The product / It	is not	sold in supermarkets.
The products / They	are not	sold in supermarkets.

Question forms

Is	the product / it	sold in supermarkets?
Are	the products / they	

Where / When	is	the product / it	sold?
Why / How	are	the products / they	

Examples

The product is manufactured in China. (Unit 29)

The vegetables are flown to Europe. (Unit 29)

The goods are stored in warehouses before they are sold. (Unit 29)

Where are your favourite clothes made? Where do you buy them? How are they transported there? (Unit 29)

Verbs 5: past passive

Form

- You make the past passive with 'was' or 'were' + the past participle (= third form) of the verb.
- Some verbs are irregular. For irregular past participle forms, see page 112.

Affirmative sentences

The product It	was	sold in supermarkets.
The products They	were	

Negative sentences

The product It	was not	sold in supermarkets.
The products They	were not	

Question forms

Was	the product it	sold in supermarkets?
Were	the products they	

Where When Why How	was	the product it	sold?
	were	the products they	

Examples

It was developed at an IBM centre in Florida. (Unit 31)

The disks were produced in Singapore. (Unit 31)

Where was the screen made? (Unit 31)

When were the first PCs produced? (Unit 31)

Where was it all put together? (Unit 31)

Irregular verbs

Base form (infinitive)	Second form (past simple)	Third form (past participle)
be	was/were	been
become	became	become
begin	began	begun
break	broke	broken
bring	brought	brought
build	built	built
buy	bought	bought
catch	caught	caught
choose	chose	chosen
come	came	come
cost	cost	cost
cut	cut	cut
deal	dealt	dealt
do	did	done
draw	drew	drawn
drink	drank	drunk
drive	drove	driven
eat	ate	eaten
fall	fell	fallen
feel	felt	felt
find	found	found
fly	flew	flown
forbid	forbade	forbidden
forget	forgot	forgotten
get	got	got
give	gave	given
go	went	gone
grow	grew	grown
have	had	had
hear	heard	heard
hide	hid	hidden
hit	hit	hit
hold	held	held
hurt	hurt	hurt
keep	kept	kept
know	knew	known
lay	laid	laid
lead	led	led
learn	learnt/learned	learnt/learned
leave	left	left
lend	lent	lent

Base form (infinitive)	Second form (past simple)	Third form (past participle)
let	let	let
lie	lay	lain
lose	lost	lost
make	made	made
mean	meant	meant
meet	met	met
pay	paid	paid
quit	quit	quit
read	read	read
ride	rode	ridden
rain	rang	rung
rise	rose	risen
say	said	said
see	saw	seen
sell	sold	sold
send	sent	sent
set	set	set
shake	shook	shaken
shoot	shot	shot
show	showed	shown
shut	shut	shut
sing	sang	sung
sit	sat	sat
sleep	slept	slept
speak	spoke	spoken
spend	spent	spent
spread	spread	spread
stand	stood	stood
steal	stole	stolen
stick	stuck	stuck
swim	swam	swum
take	took	taken
teach	taught	taught
tell	told	told
think	thought	thought
throw	threw	thrown
understand	understood	understood
wear	wore	worn
win	won	won
write	wrote	written

Answer key

1.3 Nouns: salary, money, sales
Verbs: lose, learn, sell
Adjectives: big, expensive, helpful, long, old

1.4
2 phrase	**4** phrase	**6** phrase
3 sentence	**5** sentence	

1.5
2 true	**4** false	**6** false
3 true	**5** true	

1.6 **1** I live <u>in</u> Paris.
2

Base form (infinitive)	Second form (past simple)
be	was/were
become	became
come	came

3 1c, 2a, 3b
4 1 base   2 second   3 plural   4 question   5 phrase

2.1 full-time job, part-time job, permanent job

2.2 money: currency, dollars
company departments: research and development, marketing, training

2.3 1f, 2e, 3b, 4c, 5d, 6a

2.4

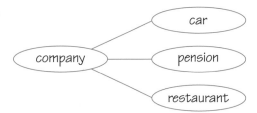

3.1 These answers are for the *Cambridge Essential English Dictionary*.
1 's' uses 44 pages (pages 276–320)
2 'x' has three entries
3 before: 'employ'; after: 'employer'
4 In the CEED, you look at the entry for 'rose' to find the verb 'rise'. You can also look at the verb table on page 112 of this book.
5 work, worker, world, World Wide Web, worse, worth

3.2 **1** five
2 heavy /'hevi/
3 an adjective
4 light

3.3 **1** yes
2 She got a job as a cleaner. I did a few jobs around the house. It's my job to water the plants.
3 make a bad/good job of something
4 no

3.4
1 a noun
2 four
3 We do a lot of business with China. He runs a small decorating business.
be none of someone's business, mind your own business

4.1
4.2

		BrE	AmE
1	432	four hundred and thirty-two	four hundred thirty-two
2	240,000	two hundred and forty thousand	two hundred forty thousand
3	191	a/one hundred and ninety-one	one hundred ninety-one
4	11,000,000	eleven million	eleven million
5	6,912	six thousand nine hundred and twelve	six thousand nine hundred twelve

4.3
2 eighteen fourteen   4 nineteen oh one   6 nineteen forty-four
3 eighteen seventy   5 nineteen twenty-six   7 nineteen ninety-two

Over to you – sample answer
2 – two
10 – ten
3,320 – three thousand three hundred and twenty (BrE); three thousand three hundred twenty (AmE)
3,000,000 – three million
55,000,000 – fifty-five million

5.1
1 third   3 twenty-ninth   5 forty-first
2 seventeenth   4 thirty-third   6 fifty-sixth

5.2

5.3

	Percentage	Fraction	Decimal
1	seventy-five per cent	three quarters	(nought/zero) point seven five
2	fifty per cent	a half / one half	(nought/zero) point five
3	twenty-five per cent	a quarter / one quarter	(nought/zero) point two five
4	twenty per cent	a fifth / one fifth	(nought/zero) point two
5	ten per cent	a tenth / one tenth	(nought/zero) point one

Over to you – sample answer
I work on the fifth floor. Ms Adams works on the eighth floor. Mr Bryant works on the nineteenth floor. Mrs Cass works on the twenty-third floor.

6.1 2 a photographer
3 an architect
4 a doctor / a nurse

6.2 1b, 2f, 3e, 4c, 5a, 6d

6.3 2 What does he do?
3 What do they do?
4 What does she do?

Over to you – sample answer
I'm a factory worker. I want to be rock musician.
Ann is a manager. Bob is an office worker. Charlene is a driver.

7.1 2e, 3d, 4a, 5c

7.2 | 1 in | 3 at | 5 in | 7 at |
| 2 on | 4 in | 6 on | |

7.3 | 1 do you work in | 3 does he work in | 5 do they work |
| 2 does she work in | 4 do you work | |

7.4 | 1 telecoms | 3 education | 5 advertising |
| 2 oil | 4 tourism | 6 construction |

Over to you – sample answer
I work at head office. Jaime works in the finance department. Sheila and Ursula work in the production department.

8.1

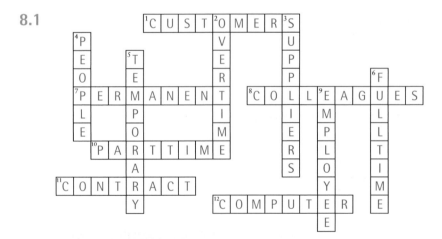

8.2

Verb	Noun
retire	retirement
resign	resignation
dismiss	dismissal

Noun	Adjective
redundancy	redundant

8.3 **1** redundant   **2** resign   **3** fire   **4** retire

Over to you – sample answer
I have a full-time job. I'd like a part-time job so I can have more time with my children. My job is permanent – I have a contract.

9.1 **1** true   **2** false   **3** false   **4** true

9.2 **1** How many   **4** how many   **7** Are there   **10** on average
      2 about   **5** There are   **8** there is
      3 exact figure   **6** altogether   **9** hours a week

9.3 **1** head office, offices   **2** branches   **3** warehouses   **4** sites

Over to you – sample answer
I work for ATR Manufacturing. Our head office is in Mexico City. There are about 15,000 employees. We have ten sites altogether in Mexico – two offices, seven branches and one warehouse.

10.1 **1f, 2a, 3d, 4c, 5b, 6e**

10.2 **1** never gets   **3** leaves   **5** stops
      2 doesn't get   **4** goes, reads   **6** walks

10.3 6, 5, 2, 3, 4, 1

Over to you – sample answer
I commute to work – I take the train. I leave home at 8.15 and I get to work at 9.15.

11.1 **2** the finance director   **3** the chief executive   **4** the sales director
      5 the research and development director

11.2 **2** The finance director is responsible for getting the money to develop and make the planes.
      3 The chief executive is responsible for the whole company.
      4 The sales director is responsible for finding customers for the planes.
      5 The research and development director is responsible for thinking of new ideas for planes.

11.3

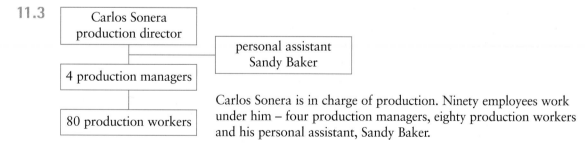

Carlos Sonera is in charge of production. Ninety employees work under him – four production managers, eighty production workers and his personal assistant, Sandy Baker.

Over to you – sample answer

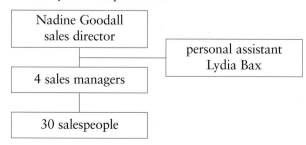

12.1

Base form (infinitive)	Second form (past simple)
be	was/were
become	became
come	came
do	did
get	got
go	went
join	joined
leave	left
move	moved
start	started
study	studied
work	worked

12.2 **1** go **2** went **3** did **4** worked **5** joined **6** become **7** became **8** move **9** got

Over to you – sample answer
I was born in 1971 in Aarhus and I went to school there. I moved to Copenhagen in 1995 when I joined Carlsberg. I became head of sales in 2001.

13.1 **1** He's (very) good with computers.
2 She isn't very good with computers.
3 She's (very) good with people.
4 He isn't very good with people.
5 He's (very) good with figures.
6 She's good with figures.

13.2 Jocasta doesn't have computer skills.
Jocasta has people skills.
Boris doesn't have people skills.

13.3 **1** language skills
2 problem-solving skills
3 presentation skills
4 negotiating skills
5 listening skills
6 management skills

Over to you – sample answer
I'm very good with computers and very good with people. But I'm not very good with figures.

14.1

BISG

290 Park Lane, London W1
Tel: +44 20 970 2000   **Fax:** +44 20 970 2055
Email: sam.unwin@bisg.co.uk

Samantha   Unwin ,   BA   (French)
Training   Director

14.2   1 experience   3 learn   5 on-the-job
          2 as   4 skills 6 training course

Over to you – sample answer
In my job – selling – qualifications are not important. You just sell the products.
You get a lot of on-the-job training. But it's good to go on training courses about the products.

15.1   1 one thirty / half past one
          2 three forty-five / quarter to four
          3 six o'clock
          4 seven fifteen / quarter past seven
          5 eleven twenty-nine / twenty-nine minutes past eleven
          6 twelve thirty-seven / twenty-three minutes to one

15.2   1 from, in the morning, in the afternoon
          2 at, in the evening, at, three in the morning
          3 at, in the morning, at, in the evening
          4 at, in the morning, at, in the afternoon

Over to you – sample answer
It's 2.30 pm now. I go to work at 7.30 am. I get home at 5.45 pm.

16.1

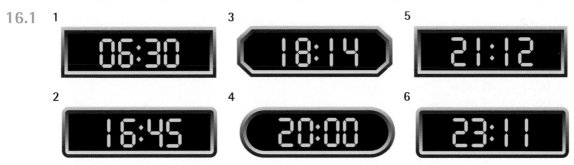

16.2   1 A: When does the train leave Singapore?
             B: It <u>leaves</u> Singapore at 08.30.
          2 A: Is it a <u>direct</u> train?
             B: No, it isn't. You <u>change</u> trains in Kuala Lumpur and Butterworth.
          3 A: When does the train arrive in Kuala Lumpur?
             B: It <u>arrives</u> in Kuala Lumpur <u>at 15.00</u>.
          4 A: <u>What</u> time <u>does</u> it <u>leave</u> Kuala Lumpur?
             B: It leaves Kuala Lumpur at 20.10.
          5 A: <u>When does</u> it <u>arrive</u> in Butterworth?
             B: It arrives in Butterworth <u>at 06.10</u> the next day.
          6 A: <u>When does the train leave</u> Butterworth?
             B: It leaves Butterworth at <u>14.30</u>.
          7 A: When <u>does the train arrive</u> in Bangkok?
             B: <u>It arrives in</u> Bangkok at 10.00 the next day.

16.3   2 A: How long does the journey take from Singapore to Kuala Lumpur? B: It takes six and a half hours.
3 A: How long does the journey take from Kuala Lumpur to Butterworth? B: It takes ten hours.
4 A: How long does the journey take from Butterworth to Bangkok? B: It takes nineteen and a half hours.

Over to you – sample answer
A: What time does the train leave Paris?   B: It leaves Paris at 14.00.
A: When does it arrive in Valence?   B: It arrives in Valence at 16.30.
A: When does it leave Valence?   B: It leaves Valence at 16.35.
A: When does it arrive in Avignon?   B: It arrives in Avignon at 17.00.
A: How long does the journey take?   B: It takes three and a half hours.

17.1   2 the twenty-fifth of April   April the twenty-fifth   April twenty-fifth
3 the fourth of July   July the fourth   July fourth
4 the fourteenth of July   July the fourteenth   July fourteenth
5 the twenty-ninth of October October the twenty-ninth   October twenty-ninth
6 the twentieth of November   November the twentieth   November twentieth
7 the thirty-first of December December the thirty-first December thirty-first

17.2   1 The Cat Show is on Monday 28th March / Monday 28 March / Monday March 28th.
2 The Business Show is on Thursday 31st March / Thursday 31 March / Thursday March 31st.
3 The Fashion Show is on Saturday 2nd April / Saturday 2 April / Saturday April 2nd.
4 The Home Show is on Sunday 3rd April / Sunday 3 April / Sunday April 3rd.
5 The Boat Show is on Wednesday 20th April / Wednesday 20 April / Wednesday April 20th.

17.3   1 in   3 in, in   5 on
2 on   4 in

Over to you – sample answer
My birthday is on the twenty-second of September. My birthday is on 22nd September.
The next payday is on the twenty-fifth of May. The next payday is on 25th May.
I go on holiday on the first of July. I go on holiday on 1st July.

18.1   2 on time   4 ten minutes late
3 half an hour late 5 half an hour early

18.2   1c, 2a, 3d, 4b

18.3   2 I usually have lunch at a restaurant.   4 I always watch television in the evening.
3 I never go skiing in winter.   5 I often go to the gym.

Over to you – sample answer
I often have lunch with colleagues.
I never go for a drink at the pub after work.
I sometimes go to the cinema in the evening.

19.1 2 On Tuesday I'm visiting a customer in the morning. I'm meeting my daughter's teacher at her school in the afternoon.

3 On Wednesday I'm working at the office in the morning. I'm visiting a company in the afternoon.

4 On Thursday I'm seeing my manager in the morning. I have an appointment with my doctor in the afternoon. / I'm seeing my doctor in the afternoon.

5 On Friday I'm visiting a customer in the morning. I'm playing golf with him in the afternoon.

19.2
1 busy	3 free	5 at	7 How
2 meet	4 shall	6 When	

Over to you – sample answer
On Monday I'm working all day in the office. I'm having lunch with my friend Jim.
On Tuesday I have an appointment with my doctor in the afternoon, then I'm going back to the office.
On Wednesday I'm visiting a customer.
On Thursday and Friday I'm going on a training course.

20.1 I go <u>walking/swimming</u>.   I like / I'm interested in <u>music/reading</u>.
I play <u>the violin / the piano</u>.   I play <u>golf/football</u>.

20.2

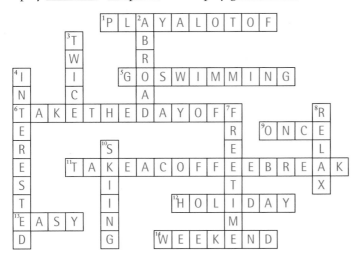

Over to you – sample answer
To relax, I go swimming at lunchtime. In the evening, I often go to the theatre. And I take a day off every month.

21.1 1 BrE: four thousand three hundred (and) eighty-four euros and fifty-three cents;
AmE: four thousand three hundred eighty-four euros and fifty-three cents

2 BrE: ten thousand and thirty-six pounds and eighty-one pence;
AmE: ten thousand thirty-six pounds (and) eighty-one pence

3 BrE: eight hundred and twenty-three dollars and ninety-seven cents;
AmE: eight hundred twenty-three dollars (and) ninety-seven cents

4 BrE: two million five hundred and fifty-two thousand nine hundred and thirty-four dollars and thirty-two cents;
AmE: two million five hundred fifty-two thousand nine hundred thirty-four dollars (and) thirty-two cents

21.2 2 thousands of dollars
3 billions of pounds
4 millions of euros

21.3   2 The price of the villa is around seven hundred thousand euros.
        3 The price of the flat is roughly three hundred thousand euros.
        4 The price of the studio is approximately fifty thousand euros.

Over to you – sample answer
The price of a big house is about €600,000. A small house costs around €400,000. A big flat costs roughly €350,000. The price of a small flat is approximately €250,000.

22.1

1 How much	3 price of	5 cost
2 is/costs	4 much does	6 is/costs

22.2

1 false	3 true	5 false
2 true	4 false	

22.3

1 of, is	3 this, is	5 is	7 is
2 are	4 are	6 of, is	

Over to you – sample answer
In my country, we pay VAT. The rate is 19 per cent on a lot of products. But VAT on books is only 5 per cent, and there is no VAT on food.

23.1   1b, 2d, 3c, 4e, 5a, 6f

23.2

1 change back	3 five/fifty-dollar bill/note/banknote	5 coin
2 currency in Doradia	4 divided into	

23.3   1b, 2d, 3a, 4e, 5c

Over to you – sample answer
In Russia, there are notes for 500, 100, 50 and 10 roubles. There are coins for 5 roubles, 2 roubles and 1 rouble, and for 50 and 10 kopeks.
The exchange rate is about 35 roubles to the euro.

24.1

Verb base form (infinitive)	Noun
cost	cost
lend	loan
repay	repayment
save	savings

24.2

1 lent, repay	3 costs	5 borrowed, repaid
2 loan, repayments	4 save	

24.3

1 sale	3 can't afford	5 expensive
2 special offers	4 waste	6 rent

Over to you – sample answer
I'm very careful with money – I try not to waste it. I eat at home because I can't afford to eat in restaurants. In shops, I look for special offers.

25.1   1c, 2d, 3e, 4b, 5a

25.2

1 company car	3 free meals	5 basic pay
2 company pension	4 working hours	

25.3 1c, 2a, 3b, 4f, 5d, 6e

Over to you – sample answer

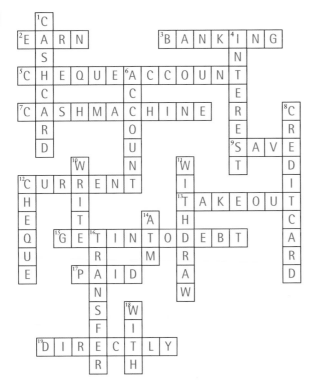

Gizmo Consumer Goods
London
Sales Director

Salary: €120,000 per year

Working week: Monday to Friday, 9.00 am – 5.00 pm

Benefits

– 35 days' holiday per year

– Company restaurant with free meals

– Company car

– Company pension

Email humanresources@gcg.co.uk

26.1

			¹C															
²E	A	R	N					³B	A	N	K	⁴I	N	G			
			S									N					
⁵C	H	E	Q	U	E	⁶A	C	C	O	U	N	T					
			C			A					E						
⁷C	A	S	H	M	A	C	H	I	N	E	R			⁸C			
			R			O					E			R			
			D			U				⁹S	A	V	E	D			
		¹⁰W			N			¹¹W				T		I			
¹²C	U	R	R	E	N	T		I						T			
H		I					¹³T	A	K	E	O	U	T	C			
E		T		¹⁴A		H							A			
Q		¹⁵G	E	¹⁶T	I	N	T	O	D	E	B	T	R		
U			R		M		R						D			
E		¹⁷P	A	I	D		A								
			N				W								
			S	¹⁸W											
¹⁹D	I	R	E	C	T	L	Y								
			R	H											

26.2

1 credit card	3 debt	5 cash machine	7 take out
2 limit	4 owed	6 cash card	

Over to you – sample answer
At the supermarket, I always pay cash. But when I buy something expensive, like furniture, I use a credit card.

27.1

Adjective	Noun
long	length
wide	width
thick	thickness
square	square
rectangular	rectangle

Verb	Noun
weigh	weight

27.2　1 wide, width　　　　3 rectangular
　　　　2 thickness, thick　　4 weighs

27.3　1 what does it
　　　　2 easy to use
　　　　3 fast

Over to you – sample answer
I have a radio. It's rectangular. It's 8 cm long, 3 cm wide and 1 cm thick. It weighs 200 grams.

28.1

Adjective	Opposite
friendly	unfriendly
reliable	unreliable
helpful	unhelpful
comfortable	uncomfortable
clean	dirty
low	high

28.2　1 unfriendly　　3 unhelpful　　5 uncomfortable
　　　　2 unreliable　　4 dirty　　　　6 high

28.3　1 comfortable/modern　　3 comfortable/modern
　　　　2 terrible　　　　　　　4 unreliable/terrible

Over to you – sample answer
I like Joe's dry cleaners. Joe is very friendly and helpful. The service is reliable and the shop is very modern. And the clothes are very clean when I get them back!

29.1

Base form (infinitive)	Third form (past participle)
buy	bought
distribute	distributed
fly	flown
grow	grown
load	loaded
make	made
manufacture	manufactured
sell	sold
ship	shipped
store	stored
unload	unloaded

29.2

1 are made 3 are loaded 5 is unloaded 7 are distributed
2 is manufactured 4 is shipped 6 are stored 8 are sold

Over to you – sample answer
My favourite clothes are made in Milan. I buy them in my local clothes shop. They are transported there by plane and truck from Italy.

30.1

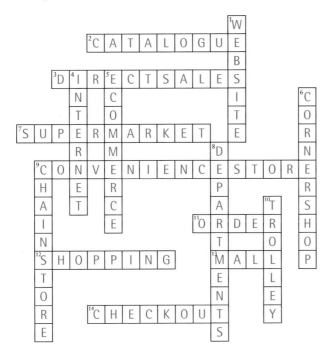

30.2

1 at 3 by, from
2 over/on 4 by, on

Over to you – sample answer
I like shopping a lot. I buy my clothes at the shopping mall outside my town.

31.1

Base form (infinitive)	Third form (past participle)
develop	developed
distribute	distributed
make	made
manufacture	manufactured
pack	packed
put together	put together
sell	sold
write	written

31.2 **1** put together **3** distributed **5** developed
2 sold **4** packed

31.3 5, 1, 4, 3, 2

Over to you – sample answer
My BMW was made in a factory in Munich. BMWs are sold all over the world.

32.1 1b Pull the lever. 5d Turn the key to start.
32.2 2c Key in your PIN number. 6f Plug the cable into a socket.
3a Put your ticket into the slot. 7c Insert your card.
4e Push the door to open. 8c Select a language.

32.3 f, g, b, d, c, e, a

Over to you – sample answer
Put your money into the slot. Press the button to select your drink. Wait for 20 seconds. Take your drink.

33.1 1c, 2e, 3a, 4b, 5d

33.2 **1** guarantee **3** call centre **5** breaks down, under guarantee, replacement
2 take it back **4** fault, repair

Over to you – sample answer
My mobile phone broke down. I took it back to the shop where I bought it. It was under guarantee. They gave me a replacement.

34.1 1a, 2b, 3b, 4a, 5b, 6a, 7a

34.2 **1** seat **3** There's **5** have **7** staying
2 something **4** this **6** been **8** like

34.3 1c, 2b, 3e, 4a, 5d

Over to you – sample answer
You: Jack, this is Susan Kelly from GJI in New York.
Susan: Pleased to meet you.
Jack: Nice to meet you, Susan. Have you been to Vancouver before?
Susan: Yes, I was here about five years ago.

35.1 a, d, e, b, f, c, g

35.2 1b, 2c, 3d, 4a

35.3 **1**

Alain:	Would you like a dessert?
Bengt:	Yes, I'll have ice cream, please.
Alain (to waiter):	Two ice creams, please.
Bengt:	That was delicious.
Alain:	I'm glad you liked it.

2

Alain (to waiter): Can we have the bill, please? (to Bengt) I'll get this.

Bengt: Thank you very much.

Alain: My pleasure.

Over to you – sample answer

You:	Do you live in Lisbon?
Your visitor:	No, I live in Sintra. I drive to work every day. It takes about an hour.
You:	Do you like commuting?
Your visitor:	It's OK! I listen to the radio.
You:	What do you do in your free time?
Your visitor:	I go fishing, and I play a lot of tennis.
You:	Really? I play tennis too! How about a game tomorrow after our meeting?
Your visitor:	Good idea!

36.1 e, b, a, c, d

36.2
1 Good morning	3 please	5 My name's
2 Hello. Can I speak to	4 calling please	6 put you through

36.3
1 phone/call again next week	3 for phoning/calling	5 Bye/Goodbye
2 good to talk to you	4 See you	

Over to you – sample answer

Rosalia Mendoza. Good morning/afternoon.

someone you know:	A: Rosalia Mendoza. Good morning.
	B: Hello, Rosalia. It's Terry here.
	A: Hello, Terry. How are you?
someone you don't know:	A: Rosalia Mendoza. Good morning.
	B: Hello, Ms Mendoza. My name's Ulf Jensen. I'm calling from LKAB in Sweden.

37.1
2 No, D for Delta.	4 No, N for November.	6 No, F for Foxtrot.
3 No, P for Papa.	5 No, Y for Yankee.	

37.2 **2** F for Foxtrot, A for Alpha, N for November, S for Sierra, H for Hotel, A for Alpha, W for Whisky

00 44 131 937 9821

3 P for Papa, E for Echo, T for Tango, E for Echo, R for Romeo, double S for Sierra, O for Oscar, N for November

00 46 8 487 5044

4 H for Hotel, A for Alpha, N for November, K for Kilo, S for Sierra

00 1 918 324 6622

5 T for Tango, A for Alpha, N for November, A for Alpha, W for Whisky, A for Alpha

00 81 42 975 2349

6 D for Delta, O for Oscar, S for Sierra, new word, S for Sierra, A for Alpha, N for November, T for Tango, O for Oscar, S for Sierra

00 55 61 648 7785

37.3 1d, 2c, 3b, 4a

Over to you – sample answer
My name is Rosalia Mendoza. R for Romeo, O for Oscar, S for Sierra, A for Alpha, L for Lima, I for India, A for Alpha, new word, M for Mike, E for Echo, N for November, D for Delta, O for Oscar, Z for Zulu, A for Alpha.
My home address is calle Kahlo 32. K for Kilo, A for Alpha, H for Hotel, L for Lima, O for Oscar, number 32.
My company address is Diagonal 550, Mexico City. D for Delta, I for India, A for Alpha, G for Golf, O for Oscar, N for November, A for Alpha, L for Lima, number 550.
My number is:

00	55	8302	9922
Double oh	double five	eight three oh two	double nine double two

38.1 1 Right. / OK. / I understand.
2 Sorry, I didn't get that. Could you speak more slowly, please?
3 Sorry, I can't hear you. Could you speak up, please?
4 Could you spell that, please?
5 Can you repeat that, please?
6 That's it. / That's right.

38.2 i, l, g, d, k, j, e, f, c, h, a, b

38.3 Possible answers:
Sophie: My number is 00 33 21 1 39 47 06.
Louis: Sorry, I can't hear you. Could you speak up, please?
Sophie: Yes, of course. The number is 00 33 21 39 47 06.
Louis: So, that's 00 33 21 39 47 06.

Over to you – sample answer
A: My name's Paul Robbins.
B: Sorry, I didn't get that. Can you speak more slowly, please?
A: I'm sorry. My – name – is – Paul – Robbins.
B: Can you spell that, please? Is that one B or two?
A: Two. R-O-double B-I-N-S.
B: R-O-double B-I-N-S.
A: That's right.
B: And what's your email address?
A: Paul dot Robbins at K-D-E dot co dot U-K.
B: Thank you.

39.1 h, d, f, k, m, l, b, g, a, j, e, i, c

39.2

TELEPHONE MESSAGE

Message for: Mary Trevor

Name of caller: Ray Bradman

☐ **Will call again** ☑ **Please call**

Phone number: 0131 899 0210

☑ **Urgent** ☐ **Not urgent**

Notes: _____

Over to you – sample answer
My name's Rosalia Mendoza. I'm calling from GIC in Mexico City. Can you ask Ms Robinson to call me back? My number is 00 55 8302 9922. Thank you.

40.1

1 written	3 reply	5 read, replied
2 received	4 got	6 fax

40.2
40.3

2 formal
Dear Ms Lumsden
Yours sincerely
Tony Kent

4 formal
Dear Ms Lumsden
Yours sincerely
Roger Olafsson

3 informal
Hi Kay
Best
Serena

5 formal
Dear Madam
Yours faithfully
Janet Freeman

Over to you – sample answer
I prefer to phone friends, to send emails to colleagues, and to send faxes to clients.

41.1   1 Thank you for   3 Could you   5 let me know
2 I'm writing to   4 I'm   6 look forward

41.2   1d, 2a, 3b, 4c, 5f, 6e

Over to you – sample answer
Dear Mr Cheng
Thank you for sending the details of your trip. Our office is near the rue Montmartre. I'm attaching a map showing how to find it.
I look forward to meeting you.
Yours sincerely
Florence Duval

42.1

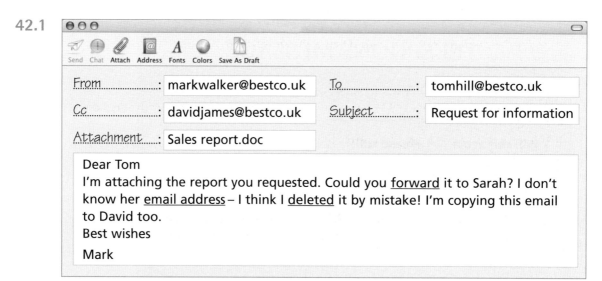

42.2   2 I'm so glad you had a nice trip back to London.
3 I've posted the brochure to you.
4 They are v. interested in working with you.

42.3   1 We are arriving in London on Monday.
2 It was very good to speak to you yesterday.
3 I hope that your hotel is comfortable.
4 I will be in touch again soon.

Over to you – sample answer
To a colleague:
Hi Steve
Here's the report. It's v. interesting.
Best
Florence

To a customer:
Dear Mr Cheng
Please find attached the report we discussed. I think you will find it very interesting.
Best regards
Florence Duval

43.1   1 about   3 for   5 about
2 at   4 on to

43.2
2 flipchart
3 check the room
4 projector
5 handouts

43.3 e, c, g, b, f, a, d

Over to you – sample answer
My name's Juana Lopez and I work for the First National Bank of Costa Rica. Today I'm going to talk about different types of lending. First, I'll talk about lending to businesses. Then I'll move on to lending to individuals. And finally, I'll look at possible developments for the next ten years. If you have any questions, I'll be happy to answer them at the end.

44.1 Possible answers:
2 As you can see in this slide of the sales plan …
3 Now let's look at Samson's branches.
4 That is the end of my presentation. Thank you for listening.
5 Are there any questions?

44.2
2 I'm sorry, but I can't give you that information.
3 If you have any questions, I'll be happy to answer them now. / Are there any questions?
4 Could you repeat the question?
5 I'm sorry, but I don't know the answer to that.
6 Can I check and get back to you?

Over to you – sample answer
First section
First, let's look at lending to businesses. When we lend money to businesses, we want to be sure that they can pay the money back. So before we lend money to them, we ask to see their accounts and their sales plan for the next five years.

45.1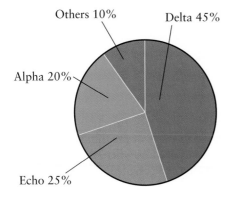

Others 10%   Delta 45%

Alpha 20%

Echo 25%

Possible sentence:
The segment shaded blue shows that 45 per cent of the cars sold in Estland last year were Delta models.

45.2

Base form (infinitive)	Second form (past simple)
decrease	decreased
go down	went down
fall	fell
increase	increased
rise	rose
stay the same	stayed the same

45.3

1	went down	3	by	5	to
2	stayed the same	4	from	6	up

Over to you – sample answer

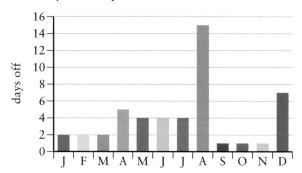

In January, February and March, I usually take two days off each month because I'm ill. In April, this rises to five days off, because I take a holiday that month. In May, June and July I take a day off each week to play golf, so the number of days off falls to four days each month. In August, I go on holiday for three weeks – so I take 15 days off. I work very hard in September, October, and November, so the number falls to one day off each month. In December, the number rises to seven days off because of winter holidays.

46.1

2	d	4	e
3	b	5	a

46.2

1 Can I ask you to keep your voices down in this area?
2 Follow me and let's go into the finance department.
3 I'm afraid we don't allow any photography during the tour.
4 On the left you can see the company's machines.
5 I'm afraid room 101 is restricted.

46.3

2	move	4	left	6	go/continue	8	restricted
3	way	5	right	7	look		

Over to you – sample answer
Guide: Good morning, ladies and gentlemen, and welcome to the DDE Advertising Agency. One hundred people work on this site and today we're going to see some of the things that they do. We'll start here in the reception area, and then we'll look at the offices where the managers work, and at the design department, where the advertisements are designed.
First, let's go to the offices. Come this way, please.

47.1

1	missed	3	postpone	5	attended
2	cancel	4	arrange	6	miss

47.2

1	take the minutes	3	attend a meeting
2	send out the agenda	4	send your apologies

47.3

1	agenda	3	attend	5	items
2	venue	4	minutes		

Over to you – sample answer

AGENDA

Staff meeting, 25 January 20_ _ , Meeting room 3

Apologies for absence
Minutes of the last meeting
1 Car parking
2 Company restaurant
3 Holiday dates
4 AOB

48.1
1 for	**3** at	**5** up		**7** in
2 for	**4** on	**6** with, of		

48.2
1 Val, can Yvonne say something here? / Val, can Yvonne come in here?
2 Val, just a moment. Let her/Yvonne finish.
3 Is everybody ready? Let's make a start.
4 Tanya and Stefan send their apologies.
5 Can I sum up?
6 Does everyone agree with the minutes of the last meeting?
7 I think that's all for today. Thank you for coming.
8 So, the first item is the company's new restaurant.

Over to you – sample answer
Chris: Is everybody ready? Let's make a start.
Chris: Tom and Carl send their apologies: they can't attend the meeting today. Does everyone agree with the minutes of the last meeting?
Chris: So, first item is the move to new offices. How are things going, Rebecca?
Chris: I think that's all for today. Thank you for coming. See you at the next meeting.

49.1 1g, 2b, 3d, 4a, 5e, 6f, 7c

49.2 1g, 2b, 3a, 4e, 5d, 6c, 7f

49.3 d, c, b, e, g, a, f

Over to you – sample answer
Rebecca: I think everyone is ready for the move.
Kerry: I'm afraid I disagree. There is still a lot of work to do.
Rebecca: Yes, but most departments are ready.
Suzanne: I have an idea. Why don't we postpone the move for a month?
Kerry: Do you mean we can move in May instead of in April?
Suzanne: That's right.
Kerry: That's a good idea.

Index

The numbers in the index are Unit numbers not page numbers.

English-English dictionary /ˌɪŋglɪʃ 'ɪŋglɪʃ ˌdɪkʃnri/ 3

entry /'entri/ 3

exact figure /ɪg,zækt 'fɪgə/ 9, 21

exchange money /ɪks,tʃeɪndʒ 'mʌni/ 23

exchange rate /ɪks'tʃeɪndʒ reɪt/ 23

excluding tax /ɪks,klu:dɪŋ 'tæks/ 22

excuse me /ɪk'skju:s mi:/ 34

expensive /ɪk'spensɪv/ 24

experience /ɪk'spɪəriənts/ 14

factory /'fæktri/ 7, 29, 46

fall /fɔ:l/ 45

fast /fɑ:st/ 27

fault /fɔ:lt/ 33

fax /fæks/ 40

February /'februri/ 17

finance /'faɪnænts/ 7

finance department /'faɪnæns dɪ,pɑ:tmənt/ 7

finance director /'faɪnænts dɪ,rektə/ 11

fine /faɪn/ 34

fire /faɪə/ 8

first /'fɜ:st/ 4, 17, 43, 44

flight /flaɪt/ 34

flipchart /'flɪptʃɑ:t/ 43

floors /flɔ:z/ 30

fly /flaɪ/ 29

formal /'fɔ:ml/ 40

forward /'fɔ:wəd/ 42

fractions /'frækʃnz/ 5

free meals /ˌfri: 'mi:lz/ 25

free time /ˌfri: 'taɪm/ 20, 35

Friday /'fraɪdeɪ/ 17

friendly /'frendli/ 28

full-time jobs /ˌfʊl taɪm 'dʒɒbz/ 8

get /get/ 40

get into debt /ˌget ɪntə 'det/ 26

go abroad /ˌgəʊ ə'brɔ:d/ 20

go down /ˌgəʊ 'daʊn/ 45

go on a training course /ˌgəʊ ɒn ə 'treɪnɪŋ kɔ:s/ 14

go on holiday /ˌgəʊ ɒn 'hɒlədeɪ/ 20

go skiing /ˌgəʊ 'ski:ɪŋ/ 20

go up /ˌgəʊ ʌp/ 45

good with /'gʊd wɪð/ 13

goodbye /gʊd'baɪ/ 34

got a job /ˌgɒt ə 'dʒɒb/ 12

grow /grəʊ/ 29

guarantee /ˌgærn'ti:/ 33

handout /'hændaʊt/ 43, 44

have a break /ˌhæv ə 'breɪk/ 20

have a day off /ˌhæv ə deɪ 'ɒf/ 20

have a holiday /ˌhæv ə 'hɒlədeɪ/ 20

have a long weekend /ˌhæv ə lɒŋ ˌwi:k'end/ 20

have a problem with /ˌhæv ə 'prɒbləm wɪð/ 33

head of sales /ˌhed əv seɪlz/ 12

head office /hed 'ɒfɪs/ 7, 9

heavy /'hevi/ 27

hello /hel'əʊ/ 34

helpful /'helpfl/ 28

here you are /'hɪə ju: ɑ:/ 34

high speeds /haɪ 'spi:dz/ 27

holiday /'hɒlədeɪ/ 25

hours a week /ˌaʊəz ə 'wi:k/ 9

How are you /ˌhaʊ 'ɑ: ju:/ 34

in /ɪn/ 7

in charge of /ɪn 'tʃɑ:dʒ ɒv/ 11

including /ɪn'klu:dɪŋ/ 9

including tax /ɪn,klu:dɪŋ 'tæks/ 22

increase /'ɪnkri:s/ 45 (= noun)

industry /'ɪndəstri/ 7

informal /ɪn'fɔ:ml/ 40

insert /'ɪnsɜ:t/ 32 (= noun)

interested in /'ɪntrəstɪd ɪn/ 20

internet banking /'ɪntənet ,bæŋkɪŋ/ 26

internet shopping /'ɪntənet ,ʃɒpɪŋ/ 30

items /'aɪtəmz/ 47

January /'dʒænjuri/ 17

job title /'dʒɒb ,taɪtl/ 14

July /dʒʊ'laɪ/ 17

June /dʒu:n/ 17

keen on /'ki:n ɒn/ 35

key in /ˌki: 'ɪn/ 32

language skills /'læŋgwɪdʒ skɪlz/ 13

late /leɪt/ 18

learn skills /ˌlɜ:n 'skɪlz/ 14

lend /lend/ 24

light /laɪt/ 27

limit /'lɪmɪt/ 26

line graph /'laɪn grɑ:f/ 45

listening skills /'lɪsnɪŋ skɪlz/ 13

load /ləʊd/ 29

loan /ləʊn/ 24

long /lɒŋ/ 27

lose time /ˌlu:z 'taɪm/ 18

mail order /meɪl 'ɔ:də/ 30

main site /meɪn 'saɪt/ 46

make a mistake /ˌmeɪk ə mɪ'steɪk/ 2

make and model number /meɪk ən 'mɒdl ,nʌmbə/ 33

make redundant /meɪk rɪ'dʌndənt/ 8

mall /mɔ:l/ 30

management skills /'mænɪdʒmənt skɪlz/ 13

managers /'mænɪdʒəz/ 11

manufacture /ˌmænjə'fæktʃə/ 29, 31

manufacturing plant /ˌmænjə'fæktʃrɪŋ plɑ:nt/ 46

map /mæp/ 41

March /mɑ:tʃ/ 17

marketing department /'mɑ:kɪtɪŋ dɪ,pɑ:tmənt/ 7

May /meɪ/ 17

message /'mesɪdʒ/ 39

microphone /'maɪkrəfəʊn/ 43

midday /ˌmɪd'deɪ/ 15

midnight /'mɪdnaɪt/ 15

minutes /'mɪnɪts/ 47

miss a meeting /ˌmɪs ə 'mi:tɪŋ/ 2, 47

missing words /ˌmɪsɪŋ 'wɜ:dz/ 42

modern /'mɒdn/ 28

Monday /'mʌndeɪ/ 17

mostly /'məʊstli/ 9

national holidays /ˌnæʃnl 'hɒlədeɪz/ 17

negotiating skills /nɪ'gəʊʃieɪtɪŋ skɪlz/ 13

Nice to meet you /ˌnaɪs tu: 'mi:t ju:/ 34

noon /nu:n/ 15

notes /nəʊts/ 23, 43

nought /nɔ:t/ 4

noun /naʊn/ 1

November /nəʊ'vembə/ 17

October /ɒk'təʊbə/ 17

office /'ɒfɪs/ 7, 46

oil /ɔɪl/ 7

oil rig /'ɔɪl rɪg/ 7

oil worker /'ɔɪl wɜ:kə/ 6

old /əʊld/ 28

on /ɒn/ 7

on average /ɒn 'ævrɪdʒ/ 9

on time /ˌɒn 'taɪm/ 18

once / twice a week /ˌwʌnts ˌtwaɪs ə'wi:k/ 20

on-the-job training /ɒn ðə dʒɒb 'treɪnɪŋ/ 14

open a meeting /ˌəʊpn ə 'mi:tɪŋ/ 48

opinion /ə'pɪnjən/ 49

order /'ɔ:də/ 5 (=noun)

order /'ɔ:də/ 30, 35 (=verb)

organization chart /ˌɔ:gnaɪ'zeɪʃn tʃɑ:t/ 11

over the internet /ˌəʊvə ðə 'ɪntənet/ 30

overtime /'əʊvətaɪm/ 8, 25

owe /əʊ/ 26

pack /pæk/ 31

part-time job /ˌpɑːt taɪm 'dʒɒb/ 8

pay back /ˌpeɪ 'bæk/ 24 (= verb)

pay cash /ˌpeɪ 'kæʃ/ 26

pay tax on /ˌpeɪ 'tæks ɒn/ 22

pension /'penʃn/ 8

people skills /'piːpl skɪlz/ 13

per cent / percentage /pəi sent/ pə'sentɪdʒ/ 5

permanent job /ˌpɜːmnənt dʒɒb/ 8

personal assistant /ˌpɜːsnl ə'sɪstnt/ 6, 11

photo /'fəʊtəʊ/ 41

photographer /fə'tɒgrəfə/ 6

pick /pɪk/ 29

pie chart /'paɪ tʃɑːt/ 45

plant /plɑːnt/ 29

please /pliːz/ 34

Pleased to meet you /ˌpliːzd tuː 'miːt juː/ 34

plug into /plʌg 'ɪntuː/ 32

pm /ˌpiː'em/ 15

post /pəʊst/ 40

postpone a meeting /pəʊstˌpəʊn ə 'miːtɪŋ/ 47

prepare /prɪ'peə/ 43

presentation skills /ˌprezn'teɪʃn skɪlz/ 13, 43

press /pres/ 32

price /praɪs/ 21, 24

problems /'prɒbləmz/ 34

problem-solving skills /'prɒbləm ˌsɒlvɪŋ skɪlz/ 13

produce /prɒə'djuːs/ 31

production department /prə'dʌkʃn dɪˌpɑːtmənt/ 7

production director /prə'dʌkʃn dɪˌrektə/ 11

programmer /'prəʊgræmə/ 6

projector /prə'dʒektə/ 43

public holidays /ˌpʌblɪk 'hɒlədeɪz/ 17

pull /pʊl/ 32

push /pʊʃ/ 32

put into /pʊt 'ɪntuː/ 32

put through /pʊt θruː/ 36

put together /pʊt tə'geðə/ 31

qualifications /ˌkwɒlɪfɪ'keɪʃnz/ 14

rate /reɪt/ 22

read /riːd/ 40

receive /rɪ'siːv/ 40

reception area /rɪ'sepʃn ˌeəriə/ 46

receptionist /rɪ'sepʃnɪst/ 6

rectangular /rek'tæŋgjʊlə/ 27

relax /rɪ'læks/ 20

reliable /rɪ'laɪəbl/ 28

rent /rent/ 24

repair /rɪ'peə/ 33

repay /rɪ'peɪ/ 24

repeat /rɪ'piːt/ 38

replacement /rɪ'pleɪsmənt/ 33

reply to /rɪ'plaɪ tuː/ 40

report /rɪ'pɔːt/ 41

research and development (R&D) director /rɪˌsɜːtʃ ən dɪ'veləpmənt dɪ'rektə/ 11

research and development department /rɪˌsɜːtʃ ən dɪ'veləpmənt dɪ'pɑːtmənt/ 46

resign /rɪ'zaɪn/ 8

responsible for /rɪ'spɒntsəbl fɔː/ 11

retailer /'riːteɪlə/ 29

retire /rɪ'taɪə/ 8

rise /raɪz/ 45

rock musician /'rɒk mjuːˌzɪʃn/ 6

roughly /'rʌfli/ 21

run a meeting /ˌrʌn ə 'miːtɪŋ/ 48

salary /'sælri/ 25

sale /seɪl/ 24

sales /seɪlz/ 7

sales assistant /'seɪlz əˌsɪstnt/ 12

sales department /'seɪlz dɪˌpɑːtmənt/ 7

sales director /seɪlz dɪ'rektə/ 11

sales tax /'seɪlz tæks/ 22

Saturday /'sætədeɪ/ 17

save /seɪv/ 24

save money /ˌseɪv 'mʌni/ 24

save time /ˌseɪv 'taɪm/ 18

savings account /'seɪvɪŋz əˌkaʊnt/ 26

screen /skriːn/ 27

second /'seknd/ 4, 17, 44

second form (past simple) /'seknd fɔːm/ 1

section /'sekʃn/ 44

sections /'sekʃnz/ 30

segment /'segmənt/ 45

select /sɪ'lekt/ 32

sell /sel/ 29, 31

send /send/ 40

send back /ˌsend 'bæk/ 33

September /sep'tembə/ 17

service department /'sɜːvɪs dɪˌpɑːtmənt/ 33

shaded /'ʃeɪdɪd/ 45

shape /ʃeɪp/ 27

ship /ʃɪp/ 29

shop /ʃɒp/ 7

shopping mall /'ʃɒpɪŋ mɔːl/ 30

sites /saɪts/ 9

skilled workers /ˌskɪld 'wɜːkəz/ 13

slide /slaɪd/ 43, 44

speak up /ˌspiːk ʌp/ 38

special offers /ˌspeʃl 'ɒfəz/ 24

spell /spel/ 37

spend /spend/ 24

spend time /ˌspend 'taɪm/ 18

spring /sprɪŋ/ 17

square /skweə/ 27

staff /stɑːf/ 25

statement /'steɪtmənt/ 26

stay the same /steɪ ðə seɪm/ 45

store /stɔː/ 29

study /'stʌdi/ 12

sum up /ˌsʌm 'ʌp/ 48

summer /'sʌmə/ 17

Sunday /'sʌndeɪ/ 17

supermarket /'suːpəˌmɑːkɪt/ 29, 30

suppliers /sə'plaɪəz/ 8

switch on /ˌswɪtʃ 'ɒn/ 32

take a break /ˌteɪk ə 'breɪk/ 20

take a day off /ˌteɪk ə deɪ 'ɒf/ 20

take a holiday /ˌteɪk ə 'hɒlədeɪ/ 20

take a long weekend /ˌteɪk ə lɒŋ ˌwiːk'end/ 20

take it back /ˌteɪk ɪt 'bæk/ 33

take it easy /ˌteɪk ɪt 'iːzi/ 20

take out /ˌteɪk aʊt/ 26 (= verb)

take out of /ˌteɪk 'aʊt ɒv/ 32

teacher /'tiːtʃə/ 6

telecoms /'telɪkɒmz/ 7

temporary work /'temprəri wɜːk/ 8

terrible /'terəbl/ 28

thank you /'θæŋk juː/ 34

thick /θɪk/ 27

third /θɜːd/ 4, 17, 44

Thursday /'θɜːzdeɪ/ 17

till /tɪl/ 30

timetables /'taɪmˌteɪblz/ 16

total price /'təʊtl praɪs/ 22

tour guide /'tʊə gaɪd/ 6

tourism /'tʊərɪzm/ 7

train /treɪn/ 10

train as /'treɪn æz/ 14

train timetable /'treɪn taɪmteɪbl/ 16

training /'treɪnɪŋ/ 14

training department /'treɪnɪŋ dɪˌpɑːtmənt/ 7, 46

tram /træm/ 10

transfer money /ˌtrænsfɜː 'mʌni/ 26

traveller's cheques /'trævləz
tʃeks/ 23

trip /trɪp/ 34

trolley /'trɒli/ 30

Tuesday /'tjuːzdeɪ/ 17

turn /tɜːn/ 32

uncomfortable /ʌn'kʌmpftəbl/
28

under guarantee /ˌʌndə
ˌɡærn'tiː/ 33

underground /'ʌndəɡraʊnd/ 10

unload /ʌn'ləʊd/ 29

unreliable /ˌʌnrɪ'laɪəbl/ 28

unskilled workers /ˌʌnskɪld
'wɜːkəz/ 13

until /ən'tɪl/ 15

urgent /'ɜːdʒnt/ 39

value /'væljuː/ 22

VAT (value added tax) /væt/ 22

venue /'venjuː/ 47

verb /vɜːb/ 1

very well /'veri wel/ 34

visit /'vɪzɪt/ 34

wages /'weɪdʒɪz/ 25

walk /wɔːk/ 10

warehouses /'weəhaʊzɪz/ 9

waste money /ˌweɪst 'mʌni/ 24

waste time /ˌweɪst 'taɪm/ 18

website /'websaɪt/ 30

Wednesday /'wenzdeɪ/ 17

weekdays /'wiːkdeɪz/ 17

weekend /ˌwiːk'end/ 17

weigh /weɪ/ 27

wide /waɪd/ 27

winter /'wɪntə/ 17

withdraw /wɪð'drɔː/ 26

word combinations /'wɜːd
kɒmbɪˌneɪʃnz/ 2

work for /'wɜːk fɔː/ 8

work in /'wɜːk ɪn/ 2

work under /'wɜːk ʌndə/ 11

work with /'wɜːk wɪð/ 8

working hours /'wɜːkɪŋ aʊəz/
25

worth /wɜːθ/ 22

write /raɪt/ 31, 40

write cheques /ˌraɪt 'tʃeks/ 26

zero /'zɪərəʊ/ 4

Acknowledgements

The author would like to thank Joy Godwin, Lyn Strutt, Sally Searby and the team at Cambridge University Press for smoothly guiding the book through the editorial process.

The publisher would like to thank the following for their kind permission to reproduce artwork and photographs.

Illustrators: Clinton Banbury, Phil Garner, Kamae Design.

Photographs: p15 bl Getty Images, tr Science & Society Picture Library, br Science Photo Library, tl Science & Society Picture Library, p18 l, cr, cl Corbis, r Getty Images, p19 tl, bl, tc, c, tr Getty Images, br Alamy, p20 tl Getty Images, t, tr Alamy/Image State, r Alamy, p20 b Alamy/Network Photographers, bc Corbis, br Getty Images, cl Alamy/Paul Thompson, p22 tl, tr Corbis, p22 br, bc, br Alamy, p24 Getty Images, p26 tl Getty Images, l Corbis, cr Alamy/Robert Harding, r Alamy/Andre Jenny, tr Alamy/Dominic Burke, br Alamy, b, cl Getty Images, p27 Alamy/Oote Boe, p28 Getty Images, p30 Alamy/Jackson Smith, p32 l Alamy/Jackson Smith, r, bl, br Alamy, b Getty Images, p35 Alamy, p34 Getty Images, p42 tr Alamy, l Getty Images, p48 Getty Images, p50 l, tl TRH Pictures, r, tr David Kimber, p50 bl Bridgeman Art Library/Ashmolean Museum, Oxford, bc Alamy/Terry Smith Images, bf Alamy/Tim Graham, p51 tr Empics, tl Rex Features/Sipa, cr Rex Features/Action Press, cl Getty Images, br Alamy, bl Corbis, p52 l Alamy, r Steve Lovegrove/Photographers Direct, p56 tl Getty Images, br Alamy, p58 t Corbis, c Getty Images, b Alamy/Jiri Rezac, p64 tl, l Corbis, Getty Images, cr Alamy/Pixonnet, r Alamy/Jeremy Hoare, cl Alamy, br Alamy/Network Photographers, b Alamy, p65 t Alamy/E J Baumeister jr, c Alamy/Ace Stock, b Alamy, p66 Getty Images, c Corbis, b Getty Images, p67 Getty Images, br Corbis, b Alamy, p68 Getty Images, p69 Getty Images, p71 tl Alamy/Arcaid, ct Dave Hebdon/Photographers Direct, tr Alamy/Isifa Image Service, cr Alamy/Carphotos, l Getty Images, r Alamy, p71 Getty Images, p72 Getty Images, p72 b Alamy/Mode Images Ltd, pp93, 94 Alamy, p100 t Getty Images, b Alamy, 103 Alamy.

Cover design by Dale Tomlinson.

Design and page layout by Kamae Design.